PHYSICS MATTERS!

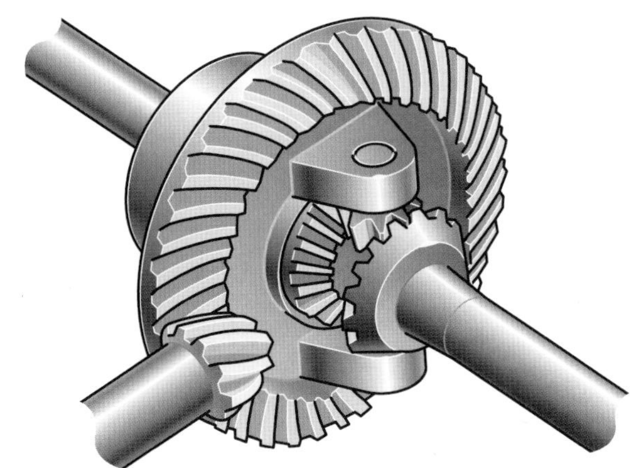

VOLUME 2
MECHANICS

John O. E. Clark

About this set

PHYSICS MATTERS! explains and illustrates the science of physics and its everyday applications. Physics is concerned with matter—the stuff from which everything is made—and with energy in all its various forms. To deal with such a wide-ranging subject in a logical way, the ten volumes in this set are organized as follows:
Volume 1—Matter; Volume 2—Mechanics; Volume 3—Heat; Volume 4—Light; Volume 5—Sound; Volume 6—Electric Charges; Volume 7—Electric Current; Volume 8—Magnetism; Volume 9—Electronics; Volume 10—Nuclear Physics
The topics within each volume are presented as self-contained modules, so that your understanding of the subject grows in linked stages. Each module is illustrated with color photographs, and there are diagrams that explain physical principles and the workings of scientific apparatus and machines that make use of them.

Pages at the end of each book give step-by-step details for activities (projects and experiments) that you can do for yourself. Each helps explain one of the main scientific principles dealt with in that particular volume. There is also a glossary that gives the meanings of scientific terms used, a list of other sources of reference (books and websites), followed by an index to all the volumes in the set. There are cross-references within volumes and from volume to volume to link topics for a fuller understanding.

Concept and planning: John O. E. Clark

Scientific authentication: Mick Nott and Graham Peacock

Published 2001 by Grolier Educational, Danbury, CT 06816

This edition published exclusively for the schools and library market

Planned and produced by Andromeda Oxford Limited
11-13 The Vineyard,
Abingdon, Oxon OX14 3PX, UK

Project Director: *Graham Bateman*
Editors: *John Woodruff, Shaun Barrington*
Editorial Assistant: *Marian Dreier*
Picture Manager: *Claire Turner*
Production: *Clive Sparling*

Design & origination by Gecko

Printed in Hong Kong

Library of Congress Cataloging-in-Publication Data

Physics matters!
p. cm.
Includes bibliographical references and index.
Contents: v.1.Matter—v.2.Mechanics—v.3.Heat—v.4.Light—v.5.Sound—v.6. Electric charges—v.7.Electric current—v.8.Magnetism—v.9.Electronics—v.10. Nuclear physics.
ISBN 0-7172-5509-3 (set: alk. paper)—ISBN 0-7172-5510-7 (v.1: alk. paper)—
ISBN 0-7172-5511-5 (v.2: alk. paper)—ISBN 0-7172-5512-3 (v.3: alk. paper)—
ISBN 0-7172-5513-1 (v.4: alk. paper)—ISBN 0-7172-5514-X (v.5: alk. paper)—
ISBN 0-7172-5515-8 (v.6: alk. paper)—ISBN 0-7172-5516-6 (v.7: alk. paper)—
ISBN 0-7172-5517-4 (v.8: alk. paper)—ISBN 0-7172-5518-2 (v.9: alk. paper)—
ISBN 0-7172-5519-0 (v.10: alk. paper)
1. Physics—Juvenile literature. [1.Physics.] I. Grolier Educational (Firm)

QC25 P49 2001
530–dc21

00-055160

Set ISBN 0-7172-5509-3
Volume 2 ISBN 0-7172-5511-5

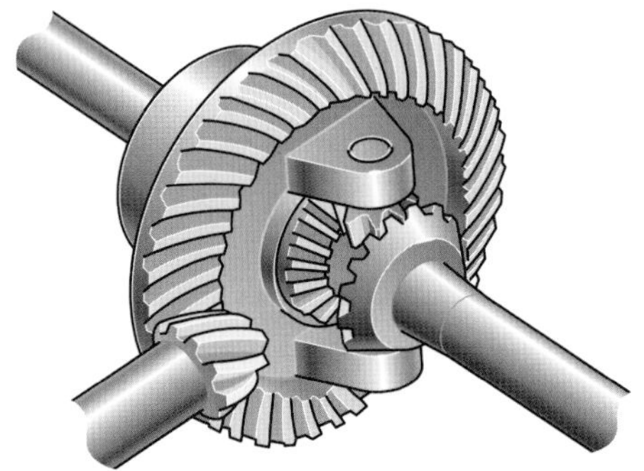

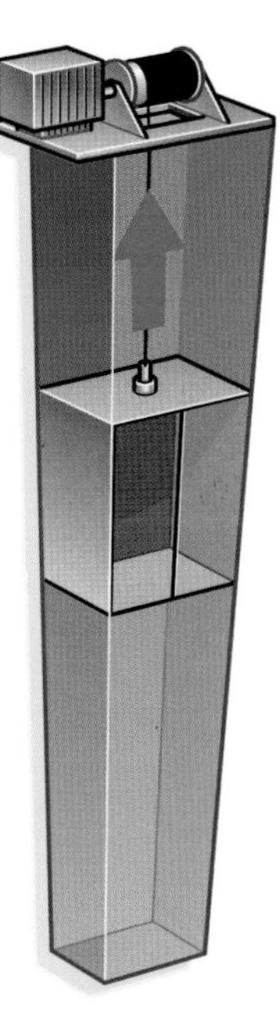

Contents

4 How to Use This Set

6 MEASURING MATTER

10 MASS AND WEIGHT

14 FALLING OBJECTS

16 VECTORS AND SCALARS

18 FORCE AND ACCELERATION

22 MOTION IN A CIRCLE

24 THE SWINGING PENDULUM

26 ENERGY, WORK AND POWER

32 STABILITY AND EQUILIBRIUM

36 LOADS AND LEVERS

40 INCLINES AND FRICTION

42 PULLEYS AND GEARS

46 PROJECTS IN MECHANICS

52 Glossary

54 Set Index

64 Further Reading/Picture Credits

How to use this set

Each volume in this set deals with a particular subject in physics. Within each volume there is a series of modular entries, from two to six pages in length. The modules are ordered so as to present information in a logical way.

All modules start with a **main entry heading** that tells you the topic of that module—"Atomic structure", for example, or "Strain on solids". A short **summary** then introduces the main text. Each volume contains **boxed features** separate from the main text, which are short biographies of some of the most important physicists.

There are two types of illustrations, each with full **captions** to explain relevance. **Color photographs** depict examples and applications of the scientific principles being described. **Diagrams** are used to explain physical principles and add to the account being given in the main text. The diagrams have their own boxes and captions. Many diagrams are labeled to help you understand what is going on.

At the end, each volume contains up to nine scientific **projects** that show the basic principles of physics. The projects are designed to use everyday materials that are easily to hand—no special apparatus is required.

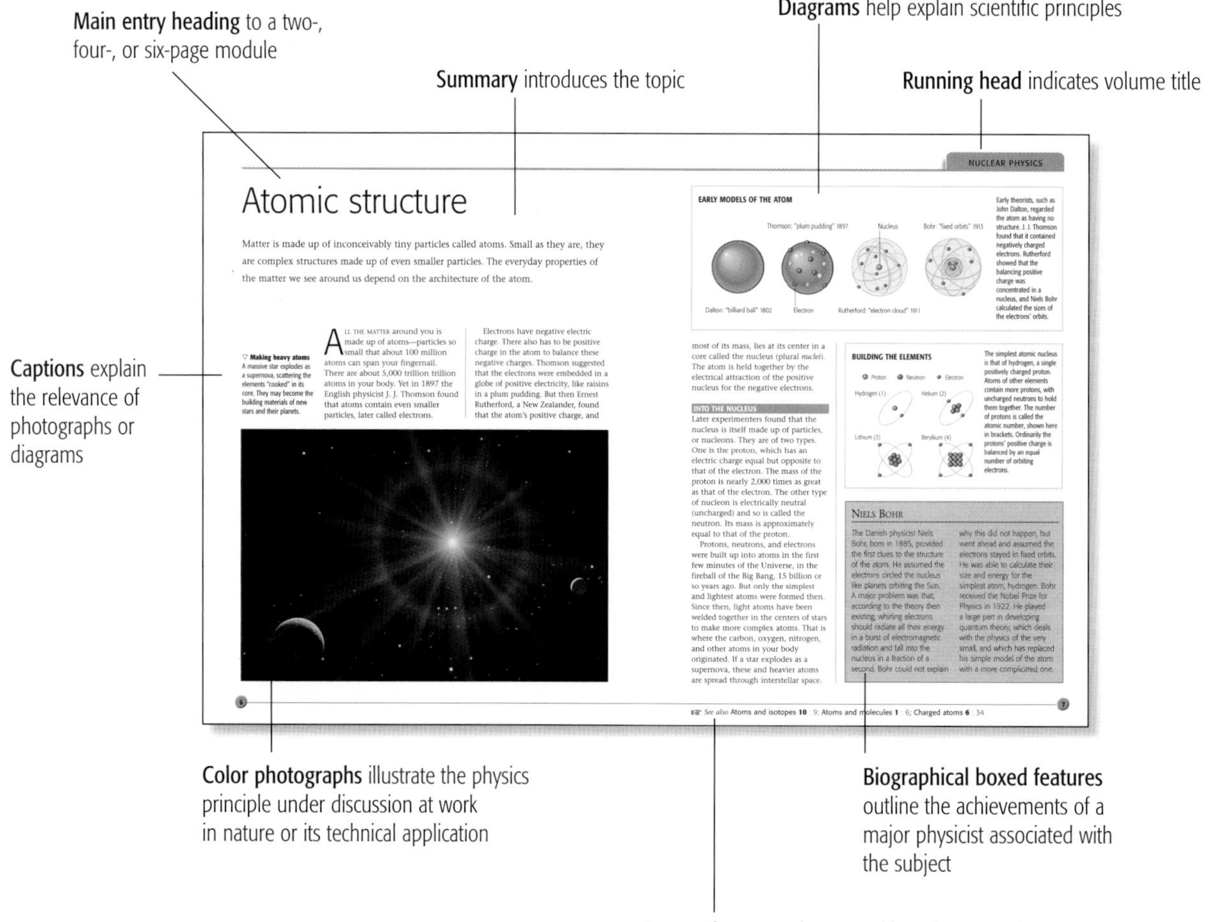
Main entry heading to a two-, four-, or six-page module
Summary introduces the topic
Diagrams help explain scientific principles
Running head indicates volume title
Captions explain the relevance of photographs or diagrams
Color photographs illustrate the physics principle under discussion at work in nature or its technical application
Biographical boxed features outline the achievements of a major physicist associated with the subject
Cross-references give entry title, volume number, and first page number of related entries
NUCLEAR PHYSICS
Atomic structure
Matter is made up of inconceivably tiny particles called atoms. Small as they are, they are complex structures made up of even smaller particles. The everyday properties of the matter we see around us depend on the architecture of the atom.
EARLY MODELS OF THE ATOM
BUILDING THE ELEMENTS
INTO THE NUCLEUS
NIELS BOHR

A number of other features help you broaden your learning. At the beginning of each module, at the bottom of the right-hand page there are **cross-references** to related entries. They are given in the form of entry title, volume number, and page. Physics has its own special scientific terms, which are defined when they are first mentioned. In addition, each volume contains a two-page **glossary** to remind you of the meanings of any such unfamiliar terms. Every volume contains an **index** to the whole set, and there is a list of other books to read and websites to visit under the heading **further reading**.

Introduction to Volume 2

Much of physics concerns the movement of objects, and in order for something to move, a force must be involved. Forces also act on stationary objects, when the forces are in equilibrium. The branch of physics that deals with forces and movement is called mechanics, which is the subject of this volume. It also includes sections on measurement, energy, work and power, as well as descriptions of levers and other simple machines.

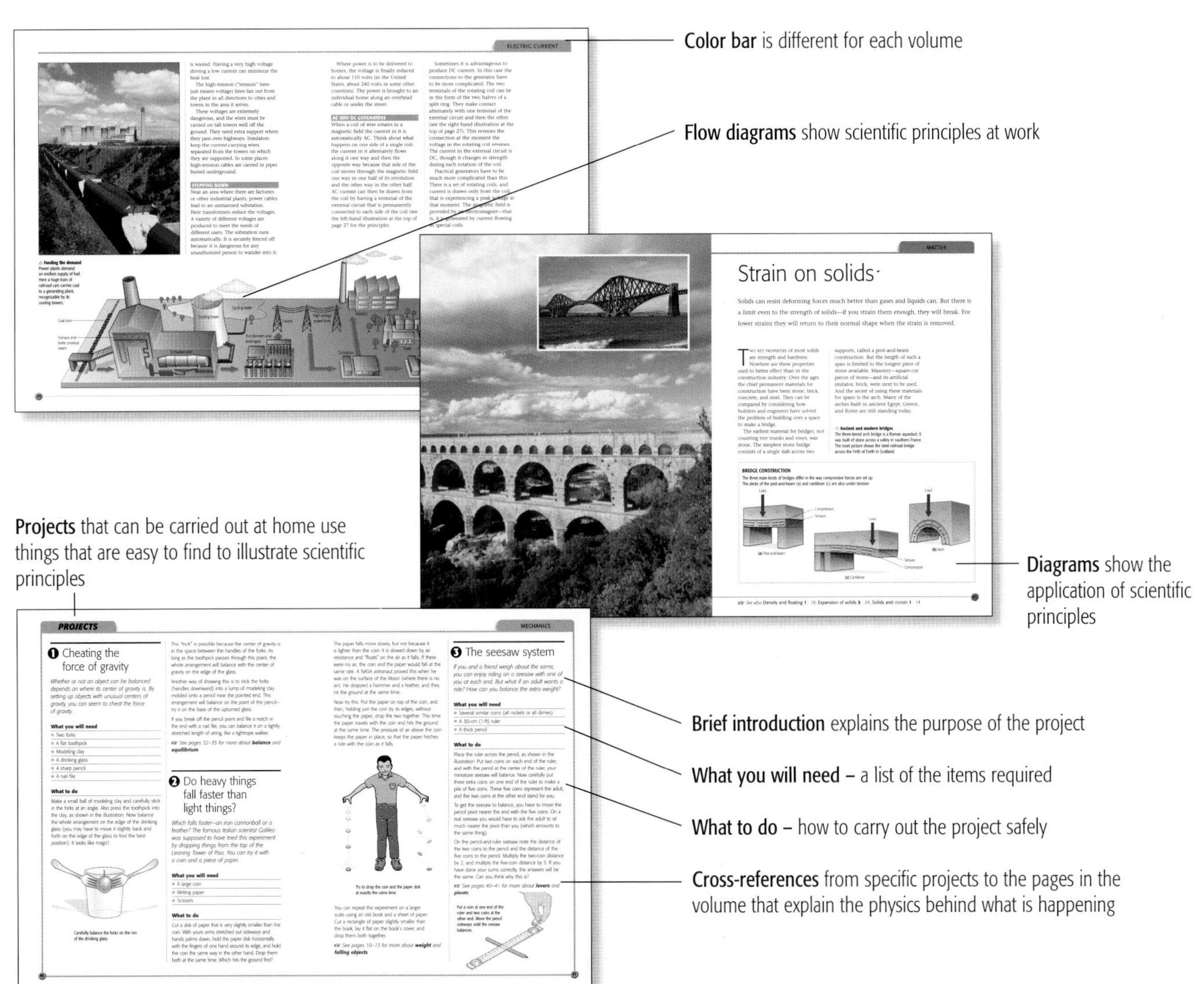

Color bar is different for each volume
Flow diagrams show scientific principles at work
Strain on solids
Projects that can be carried out at home use things that are easy to find to illustrate scientific principles
Diagrams show the application of scientific principles
PROJECTS
MECHANICS
Cheating the force of gravity
Do heavy things fall faster than light things?
The seesaw system
Brief introduction explains the purpose of the project
What you will need – a list of the items required
What to do – how to carry out the project safely
Cross-references from specific projects to the pages in the volume that explain the physics behind what is happening

Measuring matter

Measurement is at the heart of physics. Indeed, observation and measurement are central to the whole of science. Measurement requires units to express how heavy, how long, or how old something is. Science uses a wide range of units that measure everything from the size of an atom to the age of the universe.

▽ **Tiny bacteria**
These sausage-shaped objects are bacteria, each about a micrometer long. They are shown here magnified about 100,000 times.

IN EVERYDAY LIFE we use a variety of units, usually chosen to suit the thing that we are measuring. For instance, we measure the distance to the next town or city in miles, the size of a parking lot in yards, the height of a flagpole in feet, and the size of a piece of paper in inches. These are all units of length—distance is simply a length along the ground, and a height is a length measured in an upward direction.

But such a mixture of units can be a nuisance, as we find out when we have to do the math involved in changing inches to feet or yards to miles. Also, the miles used in the United States may be different from

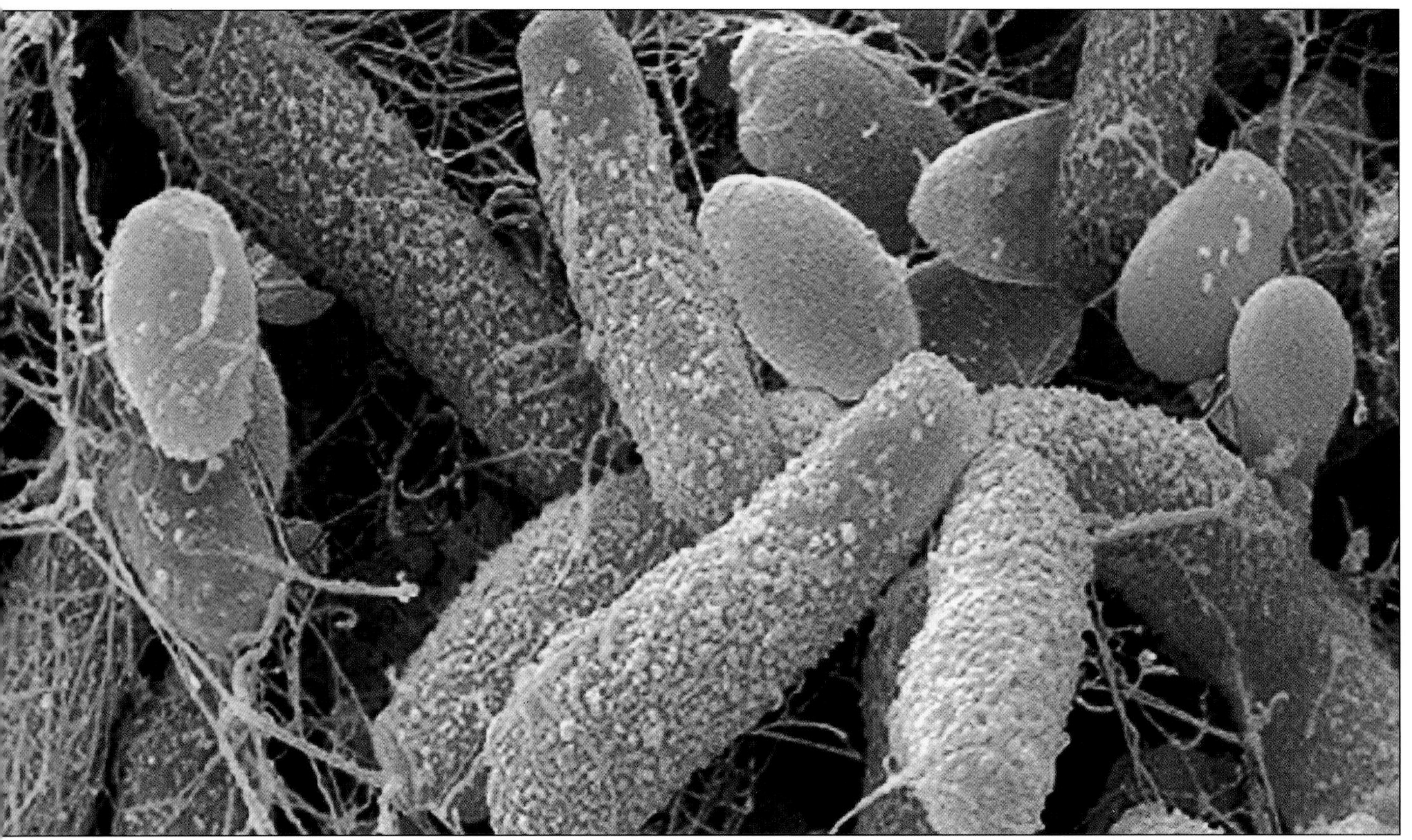

SI SYSTEM OF UNITS

Shown below are the seven *base units* of the SI system, which are supplemented by radians and steradians for measuring angles in advanced math (1 radian equals about 57 degrees). Among the important *derived units* are the hertz, used for measuring frequency; the newton, for measuring force; the ohm, volt, and watt used for measuring electrical resistance, voltage and power, respectively; and the joule, for measuring energy.

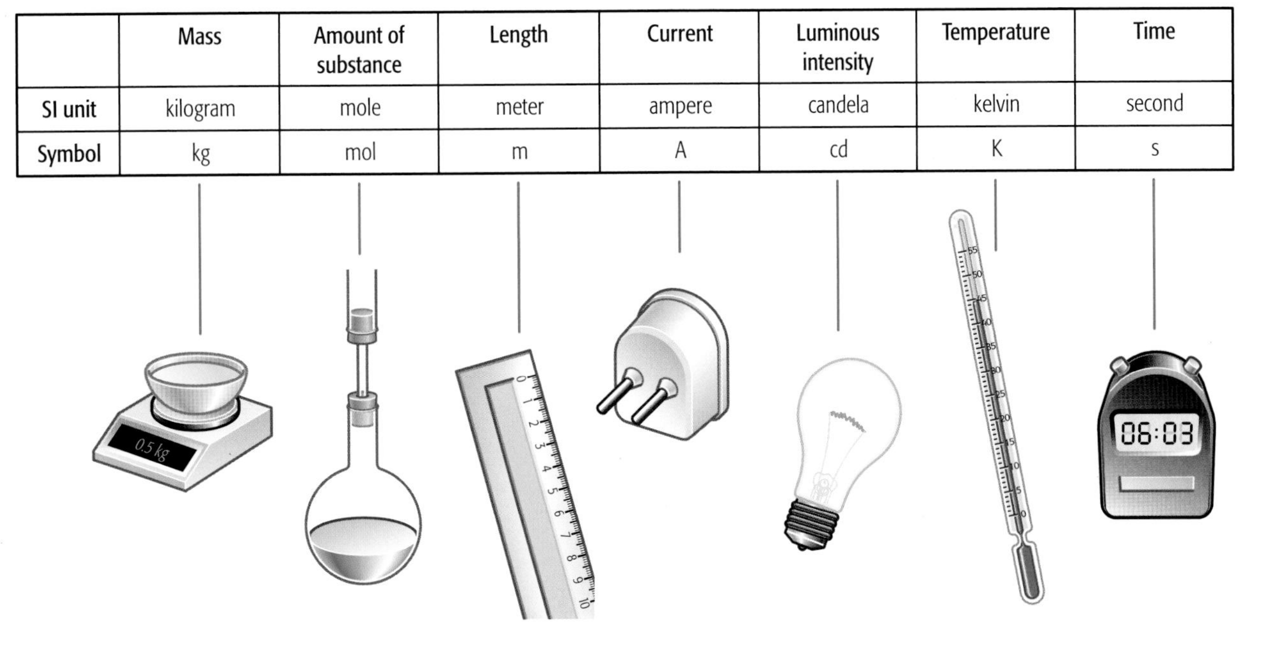

	Mass	Amount of substance	Length	Current	Luminous intensity	Temperature	Time
SI unit	kilogram	mole	meter	ampere	candela	kelvin	second
Symbol	kg	mol	m	A	cd	K	s

the miles used in Finland or in China. U.S. pints and gallons are different from British pints and gallons. 1 U.S. pint equals 0.473 liters, while 1 British pint equals 0.568 liters (the British pint is more than 1.2 times bigger than the U.S. pint). The British gallon is also 1.2 times larger than the U.S. gallon. Scientists get around these problems by having only one unit for length—the meter. Every length is measured in meters or in multiples of meters (for example, kilometers) or in submultiples of meters (for example, centimeters).

To make the multiples and submultiples there are a number of standard prefixes that go before the word for the base unit. For example, the prefix *kilo-* means "1,000 times": 1 kilometer = 1,000 meters (written as 1 km = 1,000 m). In a similar way *centi-* means "1/100": 1 centimeter (1 cm) = 1/100 meter (0.01 m). Thus the distance from Chicago to Los Angeles is about 1,740 km; the length of a new pencil is about 18 cm. There is a list of these prefixes on page 9.

THE METRIC SYSTEM

The meter is a unit in the metric system. This system was invented in France about 200 years ago, when the meter was taken to be a ten-millionth of the distance around the world. The kilogram is also a metric unit. The metric system is used for everyday measurements in most European countries and is becoming increasingly common in the United States.

☞ *See also* Atoms and molecules **1** : 6; Mass and weight **2** : 10; Vectors and scalars **2** : 16

▷ Atomic time
This scientist is adjusting an atomic clock, which keeps time to an accuracy of better than 1 second in 30,000 years.

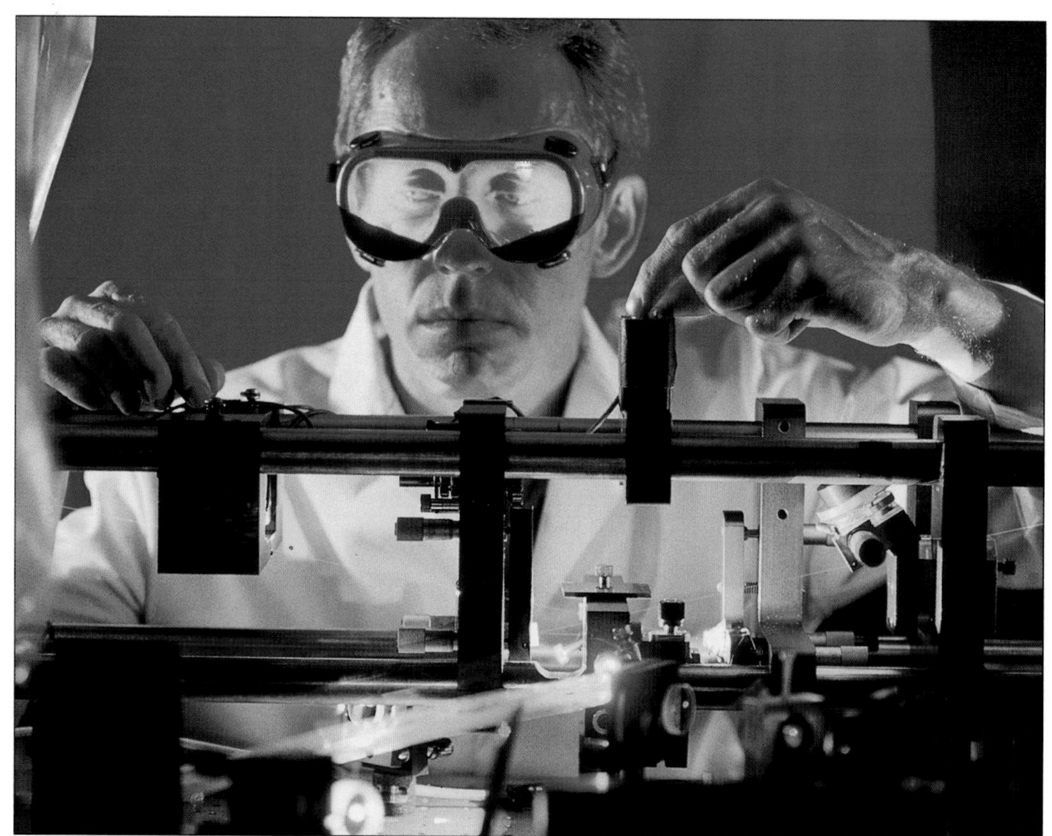

▽ Old measuring instruments
The illustration below shows some old types of measuring instrument:

(a) Human forearm, about 0.5 meter long
(b) Simple balance for weighing
(c) Water clock for telling time
(d) Sundial for telling time of day
(e) Astrolabe for measuring angles of stars
(f) Hourglass for measuring elapsed time
(g) Micrometer for measuring small thicknesses
(h) Sextant for measuring the Sun's angle in the sky

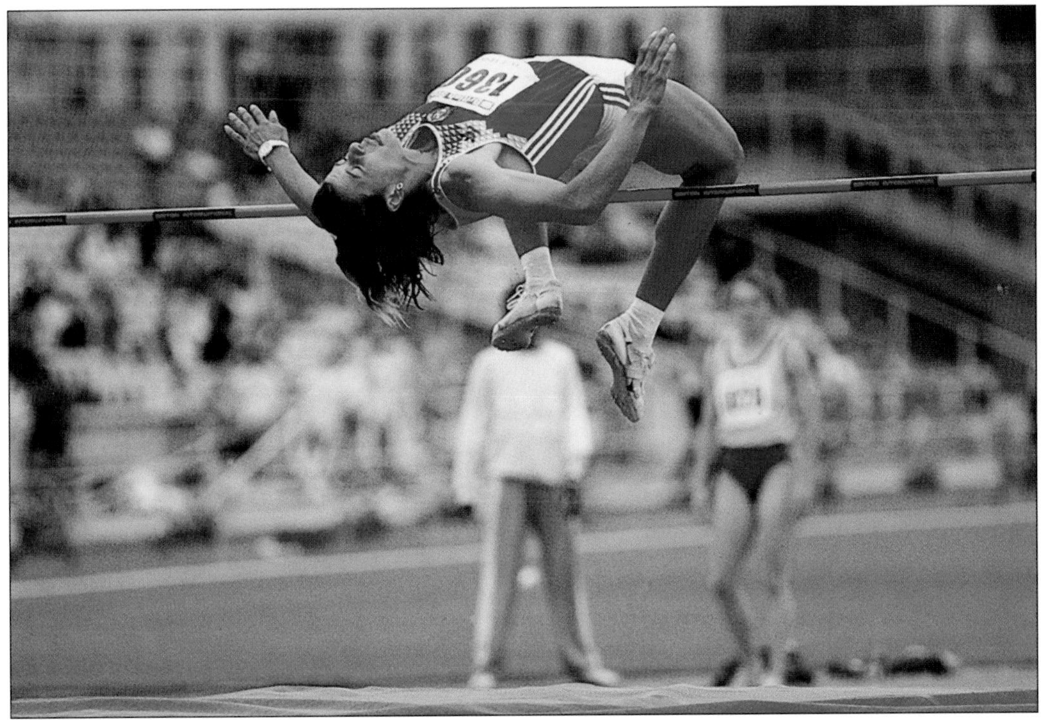

◁ **High jumper**
A high jumper clears the bar at a track-and-field contest. Athletes' achievements are measured in metric units. The world women's high jump record is more than 2 meters.

Science uses a version of the metric system called the SI system (so called after its French name, Système International d'Unités). This system has seven base units, shown at the top of page 7, and two supplementary and various derived units. There are 18 derived units, each with a special name and made from combinations of the seven base units. The base unit of mass is the kilogram (= 1,000 grams), chosen because the gram (equal to about 1/30 oz.) is too small for many measurements. Throughout this book we give measurements in SI units, usually with their customary equivalents following in parentheses.

STANDARD FORM

When measurements are made using SI or metric units, some of the numbers become very large indeed. For example, the Earth is about 150 million km from the Sun, which in figures is 150,000,000 km. *Standard form* uses an index to express large numbers as powers of 10. For instance, 1,000 = 10^3 and 1,000,000 = 10^6. So the distance to the Sun is 1.5×10^8 km. A human hair is about a ten-thousandth of a meter across, or 0.0001 m. In standard form this is written as 1×10^{-4} m.

METRIC PREFIXES

Prefix	Symbol	Multiple	Prefix	Symbol	Multiple
atto-	a	$\times 10^{-18}$	deca-	da	$\times 10$
femto-	f	$\times 10^{-15}$	hecto-	h	$\times 10^{2}$
pico-	p	$\times 10^{-12}$	kilo-	k	$\times 10^{3}$
nano-	n	$\times 10^{-9}$	mega-	M	$\times 10^{6}$
micro-	µ	$\times 10^{-6}$	giga-	G	$\times 10^{9}$
milli-	m	$\times 10^{-3}$	tera-	T	$\times 10^{12}$
centi-	c	$\times 10^{-2}$	peta-	P	$\times 10^{15}$
deci-	d	$\times 10^{-1}$	exa-	E	$\times 10^{18}$

Here are some examples:

picofarad (pF), equal to 10^{-12} farads, used to measure capacitance
nanometer (nm), equal to 10^{-9} meters, used to measure molecules
microampere (µA), equal to 10^{-6} amperes, used to measure nerve impulses
milligram (mg), equal to 10^{-3} grams, used to weigh out medicines
centiliter (cl), equal to 10^{-2} liters, used to measure wine
hectare (ha), equal to 10^{2} ares, used for areas of fields
kilovolt (kV), equal to 10^{3} volts, used for railroad voltages
megawatt (MW), equal to 10^{6} watts, used for a power-plant output
gigabyte (Gb), equal to 10^{9} bytes, used for computer storage capacity

USA
United States
NASA
2
SIDE 2
CT1 CAB 1

Mass and weight

The mass of an object remains the same wherever it is on the Earth. It even stays the same if we send it to the Moon or launch it by rocket into outer space. But an object's weight can change depending on the local force of gravity.

MASS IS A measure of the amount of matter in an object. That is why an object's mass always remains the same, wherever it is. But the weight of an object is the force acting on it by the gravitational attraction of the Earth (or any other nearby planetary body). As a result, an object's weight depends on its distance from the Earth. It is very slightly less at the top of a high mountain than at sea level. On the surface of the Moon the same object would weigh only about one-sixth of its weight on Earth. That is because the Moon's force of gravity is only one-sixth of the Earth's.

The scientific unit of mass is the kilogram (kg); the unit of weight is the newton (N). An object's weight is equal to its mass multiplied by the acceleration due to gravity (which is also called the acceleration of free fall). Because this equals 9.8 meters per second per second (9.8 m/s^2) at the surface of the Earth, there is a simple relationship between weight (in newtons) and mass (in kilograms):

$$\text{weight} = 9.8 \times \text{mass}$$

Thus a person whose mass is 50 kg weighs 490 newtons. The same person would weigh only 82 N in the Moon's lower gravity—and a huge 1,294 N on the giant planet Jupiter!

EVERYDAY WEIGHT

Scientists are always very careful to distinguish between mass and weight. But this difference is not so important in everyday life. In fact, for ordinary measurements we tend to use mass

◁ **Overcoming gravity** A NASA space shuttle with its huge fuel tanks and booster rockets towers above its massive transporter. It needs powerful rocket motors to lift it into space against the force of Earth's gravity.

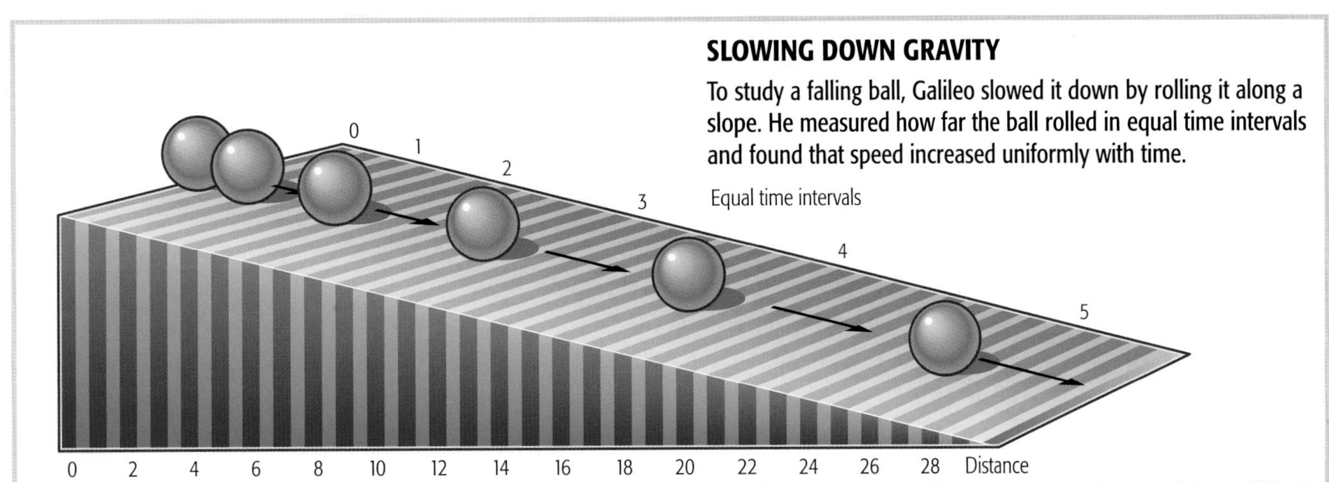

SLOWING DOWN GRAVITY

To study a falling ball, Galileo slowed it down by rolling it along a slope. He measured how far the ball rolled in equal time intervals and found that speed increased uniformly with time.

☞ *See also* Falling objects **2** : 14; Force and acceleration **2** : 18; Measuring matter **2** : 6

GRAVITY AND LIGHT

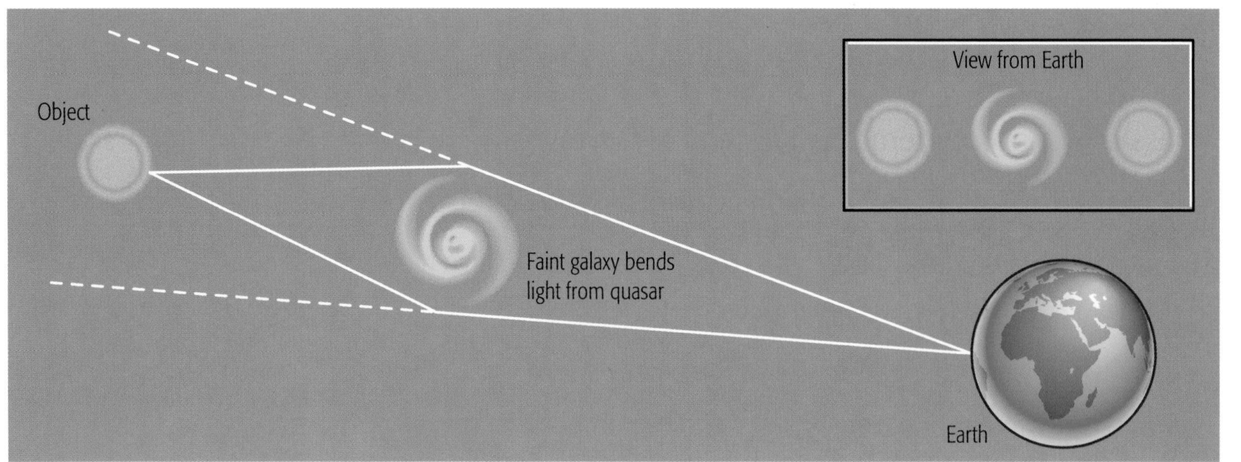

A gravitational field can bend a beam of light. When light from a distant object passes on either side of a galaxy, the galaxy's powerful gravity bends the light rays. An observer on Earth sees two images of the same object, one on each side of the galaxy. (This diagram is not to scale!)

units to express weights. Thus we might buy 5 kg of potatoes or 50 kg of coal and express the weight of the 490-newton person as 50 kg.

Sometimes we need to convert from one system of mass/weight to the other system. To convert from kilograms to pounds, multiply by 2.2 (thus 50 kg = 110 lb). To convert the other way, from pounds to kilograms, divide by 2.2.

GALILEO

Galileo Galilei, to give him his full name, was an astronomer and physicist who was born in Pisa, Italy, in 1564. In physics one of his main studies had to do with gravity. Observing the swinging lamps in the cathedral at Pisa, he realized that the regular swinging motion of a pendulum might be used to regulate a clock. He studied falling objects by dropping weights from towers and rolling balls down inclined planes. In astronomy Galileo made one of the first telescopes, and with it he discovered craters on the Moon, sunspots, and four moons of Jupiter. He also backed Copernicus and said that the Earth orbits the Sun (not the other way around, as was then believed), which lies at the center of the Solar System.

MACHINES FOR WEIGHING

The earliest weighing machines resembled the one pictured in the middle of page 8. This type, called a balance, is still used throughout science and industry. It consists of a horizontal beam pivoted at its center so that it balances—hence the name! A pan hangs from each end of the beam. To weigh out a particular quantity, say a kilogram of rice, a mass of 1 kilogram is put on one pan. Rice is then poured onto the other pan until the beam is again horizontal—until it balances. In this manner quantities of materials can be weighed out. To find the weight of a particular quantity, it is put in one pan, and known weights are added to the other pan until it balances. So to use the device for weighing things you need a set of known weights.

Of course, such a "weighing" exercise as this doesn't really find the *weight* of anything: what it does is to manipulate *masses*. This type of balance would work just as well on the Moon because it actually compares masses. But a spring balance is different. Most kitchen scales are of this type, with a vertical coiled spring and a pan on top that compresses the spring. A pointer that is worked by the movement of the spring indicates weights on a marked dial.

What this device does is to measure the effect of the force of gravity on an object's mass. It is therefore a force meter; similar devices used in physics laboratories are called newtonmeters. The spring balance really does measure weight and would register only a sixth of an object's "Earth weight" if the same object were weighed with it on the Moon.

FORCE OF GRAVITY

Every object is attracted toward every other object by a force known as gravitation, which arises because objects have mass. The force of gravity is simply the force of attraction between an object and the much more massive Earth. When you drop something, it is this force that makes it fall to the ground. The actual size of the force between any two objects depends on their masses and their distance apart. In mathematical terms we say the force is proportional to the product of the masses divided by the square of the distance between them. As a result, the closer they are together, the stronger is the force of attraction between them. If the masses are m_1 and m_2, and the distance between them is d, the force F between them can be expressed as

$$F = G\frac{m_1 \times m_2}{d^2}$$

where G is the gravitational constant. This equation is an example of an inverse square law, so called because the strength of some quantity (here, force) gets less with the square of the distance from a particular point.

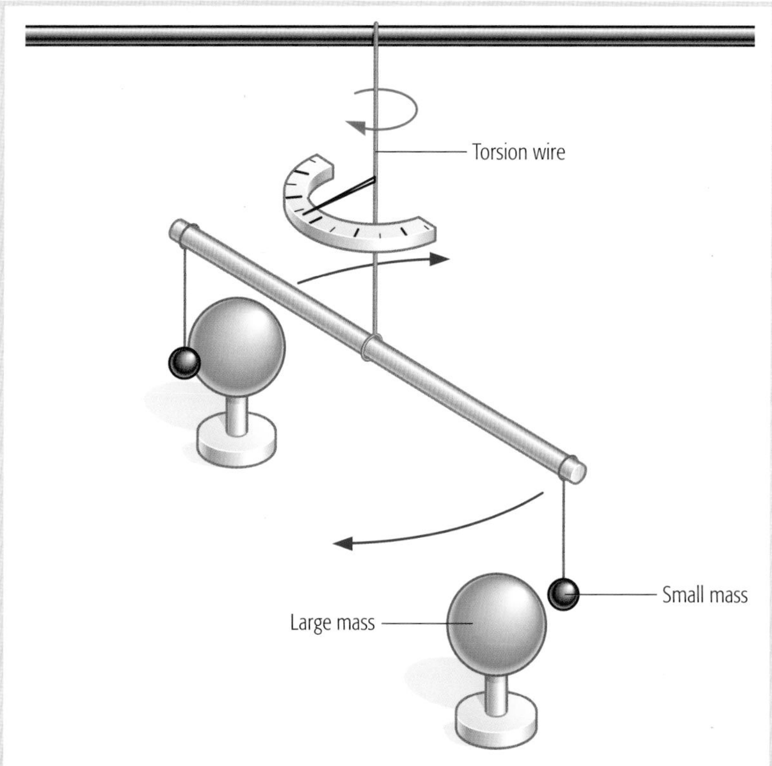

TORSION BALANCE

The English physicist Henry Cavendish made this apparatus in 1798. A gravitational force attracted two small balls toward two much more massive ones, causing twisting, or torsion, in the suspension. From the amount of twisting Cavendish calculated the value of the gravitational constant.

◁ **Challenging gravity** A weightlifter strains to lift heavy weights against the force of the Earth's gravity. He would find it much easier if he tried it on the Moon!

Falling objects

When an object falls under the force of gravity, does it fall at a constant speed, or does it get faster and faster? In other words, does it accelerate? This question puzzled early scientists until Galileo did some experiments to find the answer.

ACCELERATION DUE TO GRAVITY

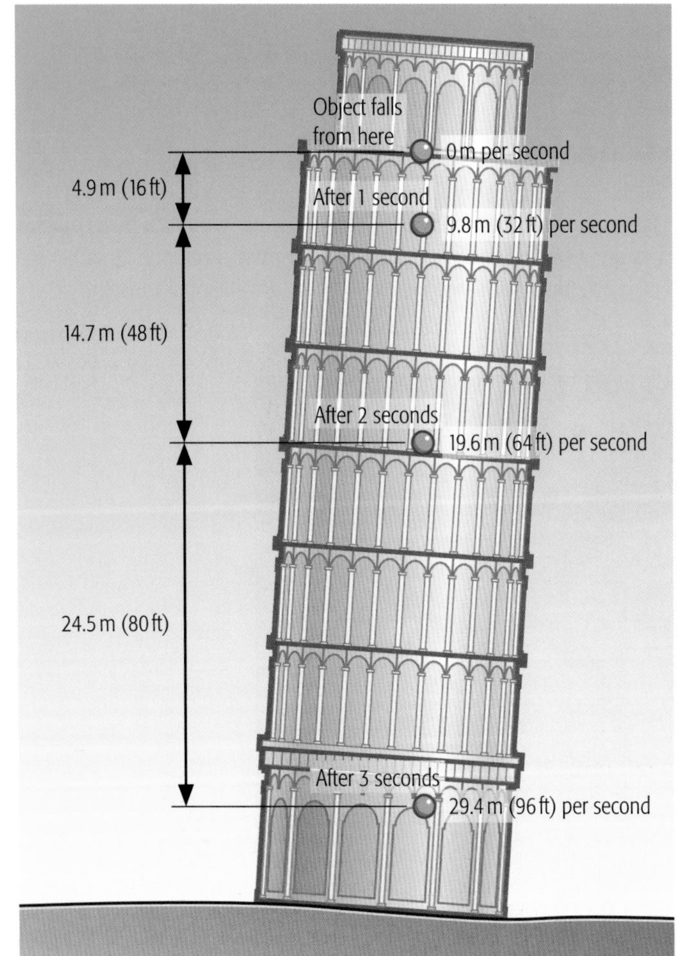

The figures show how an object would fall in the first 3 seconds after being dropped from the Leaning Tower of Pisa. Its speed increases, but its acceleration is constant at 9.8 m/s^2 (32 ft/s^2).

GALILEO'S EXPERIMENT illustrated on page 11 shows how he found that the speed of a ball rolling down a slope continues to increase—in other words, it accelerates. Galileo also found that every freely falling object has the same acceleration. Now called the acceleration due to gravity, it has the value 9.8 m/s^2 (32 ft/s^2).

According to tradition, Galileo also tried to measure the acceleration of a cannonball dropped off the top of the Leaning Tower of Pisa. The illustration on the left shows what the results would have been if he had a way of making such measurements (which he did not). The cannonball would have reached a speed of 9.8 m/s (32 ft/s) after 1 second, a speed of 19.6 m/s (64 ft/s) after 2 seconds, and so on. The speed increases, but the acceleration is unchanging.

TERMINAL SPEED

In practice, an object falling in air does not keep getting faster and faster. The air resists the downward movement of the object, and this air resistance acts as an upward force called drag. The drag increases as the object's speed increases, so that eventually the object can go no faster. Most falling objects reach a constant

terminal speed of about 54 m/s (177 ft/s or about 120 mph). Think of the damage hailstones could do if they fell any faster!

Drag is larger on an object with a large area than it is on one with a small area. This is the principle of a parachute, which when open gives a falling human a terminal speed of 6.3 m/s (nearly 21 ft/s or 14 mph). That is the speed at which a parachutist hits the ground. You can prove the principle with a sheet of paper. Drop it, and it flutters to the ground because of the high drag acting on it. But crumple it into a tight ball, and you will find that it falls much quicker because there is much less drag.

FREE FALL

An object falling under the force of gravity is said to be in free fall (and acceleration due to gravity is also known as acceleration of free fall). It has the symbol *g*, and it crops up in many of the physical formulas that have to do with mechanics, such as the formula for calculating the time of a pendulum's swing (see page 25) and equations for calculating pressures under water.

△ **Speeding skydivers**
Skydivers reach their terminal speed (about 54 m/s) after about 12 seconds. They then fall at this constant speed until they open their parachutes and rapidly decelerate, reaching the ground at a speed of 6.3 m/s.

☞ *See also* Force and acceleration **2** : 18; Mass and weight **2** : 10; Motion in a circle **2** : 22

Vectors and scalars

Most quantities in physics are expressed as a number and some unit, such as 25 kg or 110 volts. These last examples are called scalars. But what is the difference between a speed of 50 km/h and a velocity of 50 km/h in the direction of Chicago? The first (speed) is a scalar, but the second (velocity) is a vector quantity.

A VECTOR QUANTITY always has its direction specified, whereas a scalar is a pure number. A given quantity can be either, and sometimes the difference is very important. If you told some shipwrecked sailors on a life raft that there was an island only 3 kilometers away, they might be relieved. But it would be much more useful for them to know that there was an island 3 kilometers away *to the north*. They would then know which way to paddle the life raft. We call "3 kilometers away" a scalar quantity; "3 kilometers away to the north" is a vector. Several quantities in physics are vectors. They include velocity, acceleration, and most forces.

ADDING VECTORS

Adding scalar quantities is easy as long as you can do simple math.

▷ Vector positions
Air-traffic controllers use vectors to indicate the positions of airplanes. They need to known how far away the airplanes are and in what direction. Often the vectors are plotted on a radar screen.

TRIANGLES AND PARALLELOGRAMS

The triangle of vectors (right) shows how to add vectors, in this case two forces. The effect of combining a force F_1 in one direction and another force F_2 in a different direction (the lengths of the arrows indicate the sizes of the forces) is called the resultant. The third side of the triangle shows the resultant's size and direction.

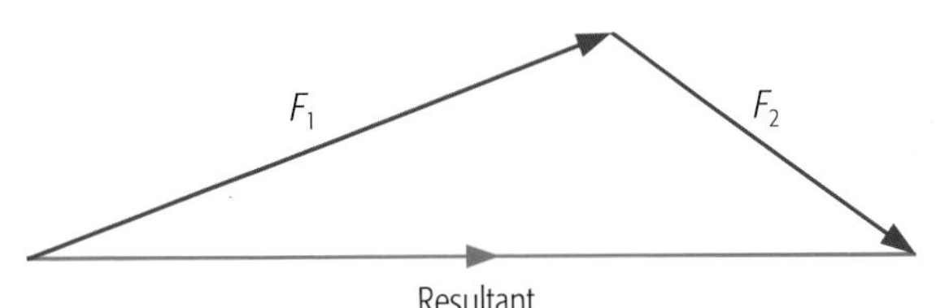

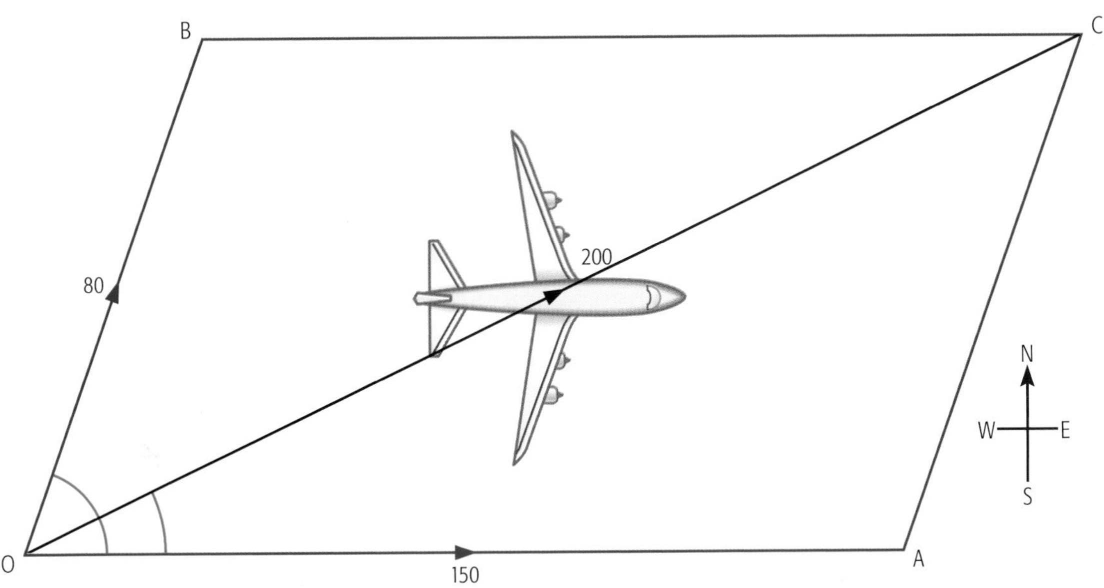

Problem: an airplane navigator wants to fly a plane 200 km from O to C. But there is a northerly wind along the line from O to B. What course should the navigator set? The correct course is due east, toward A. The parallelogram of vectors shows that the plane will actually fly along the line from O to C, as required.

A piece of string 3 meters long added to a piece 4 meters long gives a total length of 7 meters of string (ignoring the string used to tie the knot).

But adding vectors is trickier. If you push a cart 30 meters to the east and then 40 meters to the south, where does the cart end up? The answer is 50 meters away from where you started, in a more or less south-easterly direction. Notice that the cart does not finish up 70 meters away, which is the result you would get if you merely added the two distances.

DRAWING CONCLUSIONS

One way of adding vectors is to draw a plan. Make the length of a line stand for the size of the vector, and draw it in the correct direction. Then, from the end of the first line draw a second line in the direction of the second vector, again with length standing for size. A line drawn between the beginning of the first line and the end of the second one represents the sum of the vectors and its direction. The construction you have made is called a triangle of vectors.

☞ *See also* Force and acceleration **2** : 18; Measuring matter **2** : 6; Motion in a circle **2** : 22

Force and acceleration

Force is what makes a thing move or stops it. The ease with which something moves depends on its mass. A moving object has a certain speed, and if its speed changes it accelerates. Force, mass, and acceleration are interconnected.

▽ **First law of motion**
When the hockey player hits the puck, it skates across the ice and–according to Newton's laws–would go on forever if the force of friction did not slow it down.

FORCE CAN MAKE things move, stop moving, move faster or slower, or change the direction in which they move. It can also make things change shape, perhaps by squeezing them or stretching them. If you stretch a rubber band or snap a pencil you are using force. Even a humble paper clip exerts a force when it holds two pieces of paper together.

All the forces mentioned so far have to do with objects in contact with one another. But there are other forces that act at a distance. As we saw earlier, gravity is a force that pulls things down to the surface of the Earth. A magnet exerts a force when it picks up an iron nail. There are also forces that act between electric charges. In fact, nearly all of physics is concerned with forces of one sort or another. But forces are most obvious when they have to do with movement, with what scientists call motion.

THE LAWS OF MOTION

If you roll a ball along the ground, it does not keep on rolling forever but soon slows down and stops. Have you ever wondered why? In the 17th century the English scientist Isaac Newton wondered why and came up with a set of rules that apply to all moving objects. Together, these rules are now known as Newton's laws of motion.

The first law states that an object at rest will stay at rest, or a moving object will go on moving, unless a force acts on it. So according to Newton, our ball started rolling because we gave it a push—we applied a force. It then stopped rolling because it was acted on by another force. In this case the second force was friction between the ball and the ground. That is why a ball will roll farther on a smooth surface than it will on a rough one—try rolling a marble across a

◁ **Action and reaction** A person firing a rifle demonstrates the third law of motion. When the rifle is fired, a force (the action) speeds the bullet forward. At the same time the shooter feels a sudden recoil (the reaction) as the rifle is pushed backward.

wooden floor (low friction) and across a carpet (high friction).

Newton's second law of motion involves acceleration, which is the rate at which a moving object changes speed. The law says that the force acting on an object is equal to its mass multiplied by its acceleration. So if you give something a push (apply a force), it will move off at a certain speed. But if you want it to move faster and faster, you have to keep on applying force. A spacecraft returning to the Earth from the Moon travels at a fairly constant speed until it gets close to the Earth. Then the Earth's gravity (a force) has more effect and makes it accelerate. Strictly speaking, we should use the term velocity instead of speed (velocity is speed in a specified direction).

The third law of motion concerns two objects. It states that when one object exerts a force on another, the second object exerts the same force on the first but in the opposite direction. The first force is an action and the second a reaction, and the law is sometimes stated as "action and reaction are equal and opposite."

When we drop a book, gravity is the action force that makes it fall. There is also an equal reaction force between the book and the Earth, but it is undetectable because the mass of the Earth is huge compared with that of the book. The forces between the Earth and the Moon are easier to understand. The Earth's gravity pulls on the Moon and keeps it in orbit. The Moon's gravity pulls on the water in the Earth's oceans and causes the daily tides.

Another example of the third law is the principle of the rocket. The hot

Isaac Newton

Sir Isaac Newton (1642–1727) was an English mathematician, astronomer, and physicist. He was born at Woolsthorpe in Lincolnshire and in 1661 went to study at Cambridge University. In 1669 he became professor of mathematics there. In mathematics Newton developed calculus, a system that can deal with changing quantities. In astronomy he made one of the first reflecting telescopes and worked out how the Moon orbits the Earth. To do this, he used the law of gravitation, one of his major contributions to physics. He studied light and produced the Sun's spectrum by passing sunlight through a glass prism. He also formulated his three famous laws of motion. In 1705 he became the first scientist ever to be knighted. He is buried in Westminster Abbey and is regarded as one of the world's greatest scientists.

☞ *See also* Falling objects **2** : 14; Mass and weight **2** : 10; Motion in a circle **2** : 22

burning gases in a rocket expand and push in all directions. Those that push on the closed front end of the rocket are balanced by a reaction, which acts in the opposite direction and propels the rocket along. For this reason a rocket is known technically as a type of reaction motor.

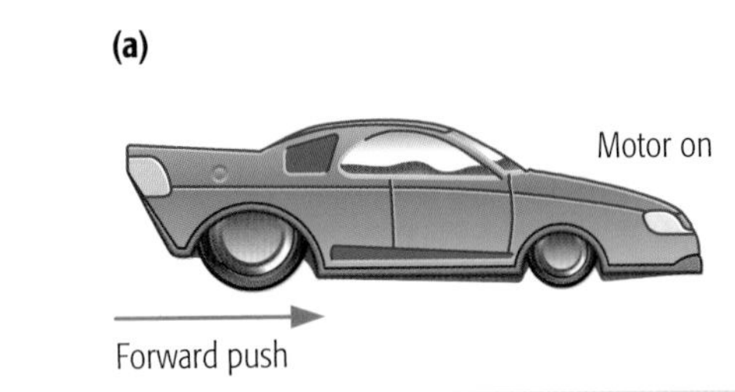

INERTIA AND MOMENTUM

A heavy object is more difficult to start moving than a lighter one. That is because of its mass or inertia. Inertia can be thought of as an object's reluctance to move. If you are traveling in an automobile and the driver brakes suddenly, it is your inertia that makes you keep moving unless held back by a seat belt.

Once an object is moving, it has momentum, which is equal to its mass multiplied by its velocity. The more massive a moving object is, or the faster it moves, the greater is its momentum.

It is easy to demonstrate the difference between inertia and momentum. If you carefully place a brick on your foot, it is difficult to raise your toes—that's inertia. But if you dropped the brick on your foot, it would do a lot of damage—that's momentum!

A small object moving very fast can have more momentum than a massive object moving slowly. For example, a bullet fired from a Magnum revolver can have enough momentum to stop a moving automobile because the bullet's momentum is greater than that of the car.

Newton's second and third laws of motion predict that when two objects bump into each other, their total momentum after impact is the same as it was before impact. This statement is often called the principle of conservation of momentum.

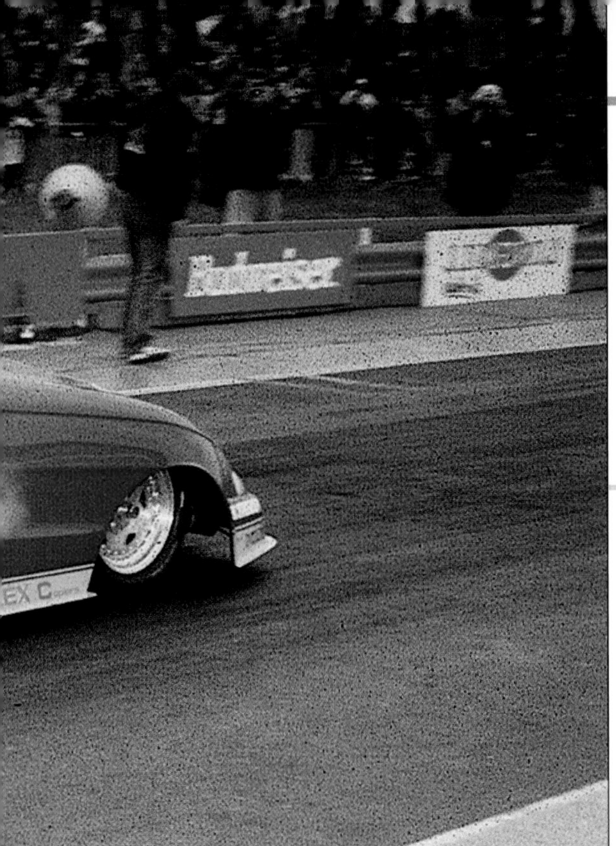

◁ **Fast and furious**
A drag racing car accelerates to speeds of up to 400 km/h from a standing start over a distance of just 400 meters (the world record is more than 500 km/h).

STARTING AND STOPPING

When the drag racing car starts (a), the forward push of the car's motor has to overcome friction. During the run (b) the car continues to accelerate as the motor continues to provide forward force. At the end of the run (c) the driver turns off the motor and releases a parachute to provide even more wind resistance and slow down the car until it comes to a standstill.

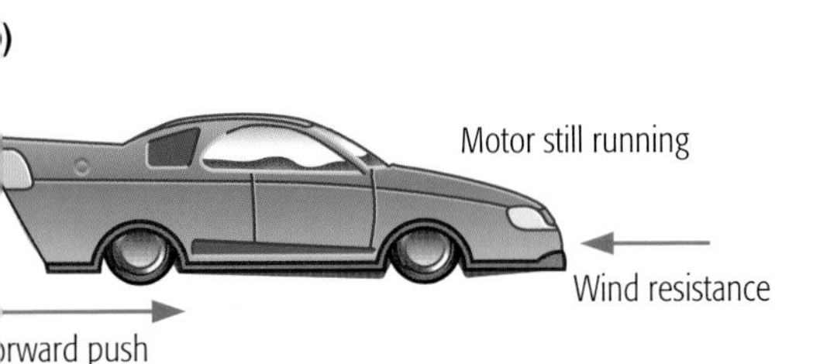

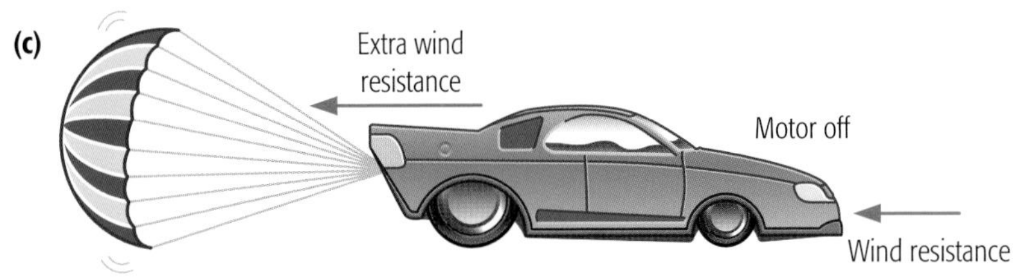

It accounts for various things in everyday life, particularly in sports. People playing pool or hockey make unconscious use of the conservation of momentum when they strike a ball or the puck. When a rider's horse refuses to jump over a fence, the horse stops, but momentum keeps the rider going, sometimes with a painful result.

Like velocity, acceleration is a vector quantity. It is specified by a number (how large it is) and a direction. An example of a velocity is "5 meters per second northward." Acceleration is measured in units such as meters per second per second. Speed, on the other hand, is a scalar quantity. It is stated merely as a number and unit with no direction, such as "500 km/h."

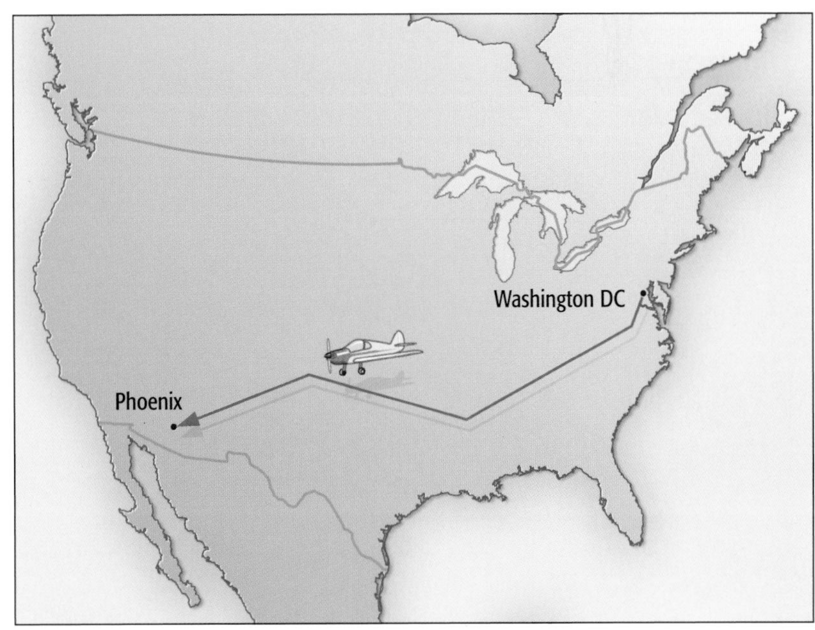

△ **Speed and velocity**
An airplane flies from Washington DC to Phoenix at a constant speed, but its velocity changes every time it changes direction.

Motion in a circle

So far we have considered mainly objects moving in straight lines and the various forces that can act on them. Slightly different rules apply if an object is moving in a curved path, particularly if it is moving around and around in a circle.

▽ **Centripetal attraction**
People on this carnival ride feel as though they are being flung outward. In fact, their velocity constantly changes as they go around in a circle.

WE ARE GOING to begin with a very difficult idea. When an object moves in a straight line, the only way it can accelerate (or decelerate) is by changing its speed—by going faster (or slower). But we know from pages 16–17 that velocity is a vector quantity. So if an object is moving at a certain speed in a certain direction (that is, if it has a certain velocity), it can be acted on by a force—for example, by giving it a sideways push—that changes its direction without changing its speed. As a result, *its velocity changes.* And that amounts to saying that *it undergoes acceleration,* which after all is defined as change in velocity divided by time. So, although it might seem unlikely at first, it is quite possible for something to be accelerating without its speed changing.

Now think of a stone tied to the end of a piece of string and whirled around your head in a horizontal circle. Its speed is constant; but because its direction is continuously changing, it is always accelerating. The force that accelerates the stone is the pull in the string. Its direction is at right angles to the direction of the stone at any instant, directed inward toward the center of the circle. Physicists call it centripetal force.

MOONS AND SATELLITES

The English scientist Isaac Newton worked out that a force is involved in keeping an object moving in a circle around another object. So what is the force that keeps the Moon orbiting the Earth? It is the force of gravity between the Earth and the

△ **Rings of particles**
The rings around the planet Saturn consist of millions of orbiting icy particles held in position by the planet's gravitational field.

FEEDBACK CONTROL

A mechanism for controlling the speed of an engine, called a governor, makes use of circular motion. The vertical shaft is turned by a belt (1) driven by the machine. As it turns, the weights (2), attached at the top of the shaft, go around and rise (3). This action raises the rod (4), which reduces the power supply to the engine and slows it down. As it slows, the weights fall and so increase the power to the engine.

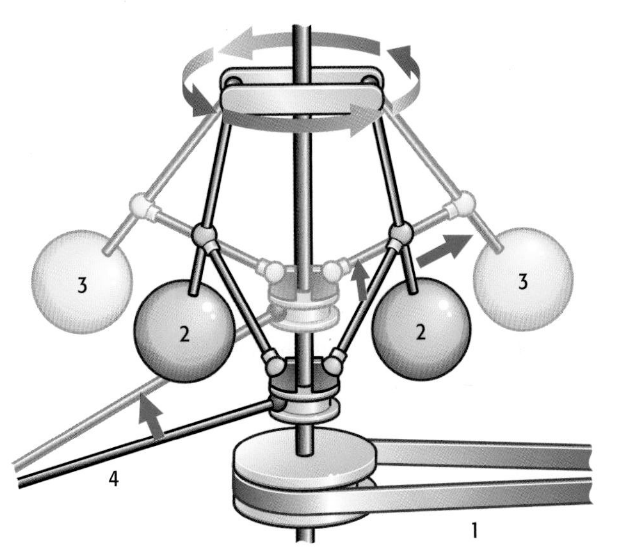

Moon. In a way, the Moon is always falling in a circle toward the Earth. But it keeps falling past and going around again—or at least it has for the last $4\frac{1}{2}$ billion years or so!

Artificial satellites orbiting the Moon, Earth, or another planet act in the same way under the gravitational attraction of the body that they orbit. To lift an orbiting satellite into a higher orbit, it has to be given more speed (by firing its rocket motors). When a satellite slows down, perhaps because of friction between it and the outer layers of the Earth's atmosphere, it can no longer stay in its orbit and soon spirals down toward the Earth.

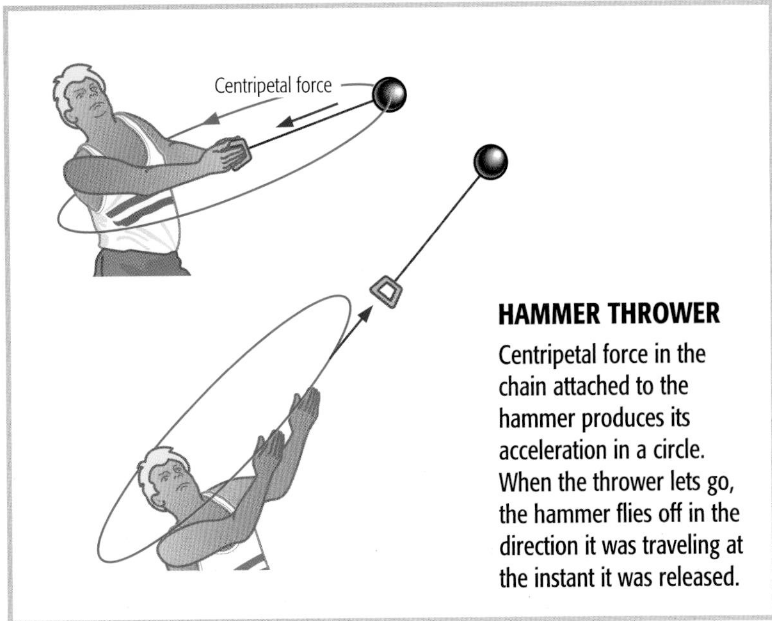

HAMMER THROWER

Centripetal force in the chain attached to the hammer produces its acceleration in a circle. When the thrower lets go, the hammer flies off in the direction it was traveling at the instant it was released.

☞ *See also* Falling objects **2** : 14; Force and acceleration **2** : 18; The swinging pendulum **2** : 24

The swinging pendulum

A pendulum swings through an arc of a circle, with the suspension point at the center of the circle. Two quantities that can be varied are the length of the pendulum and the mass of the pendulum bob. Only one of them affects the time of the swing.

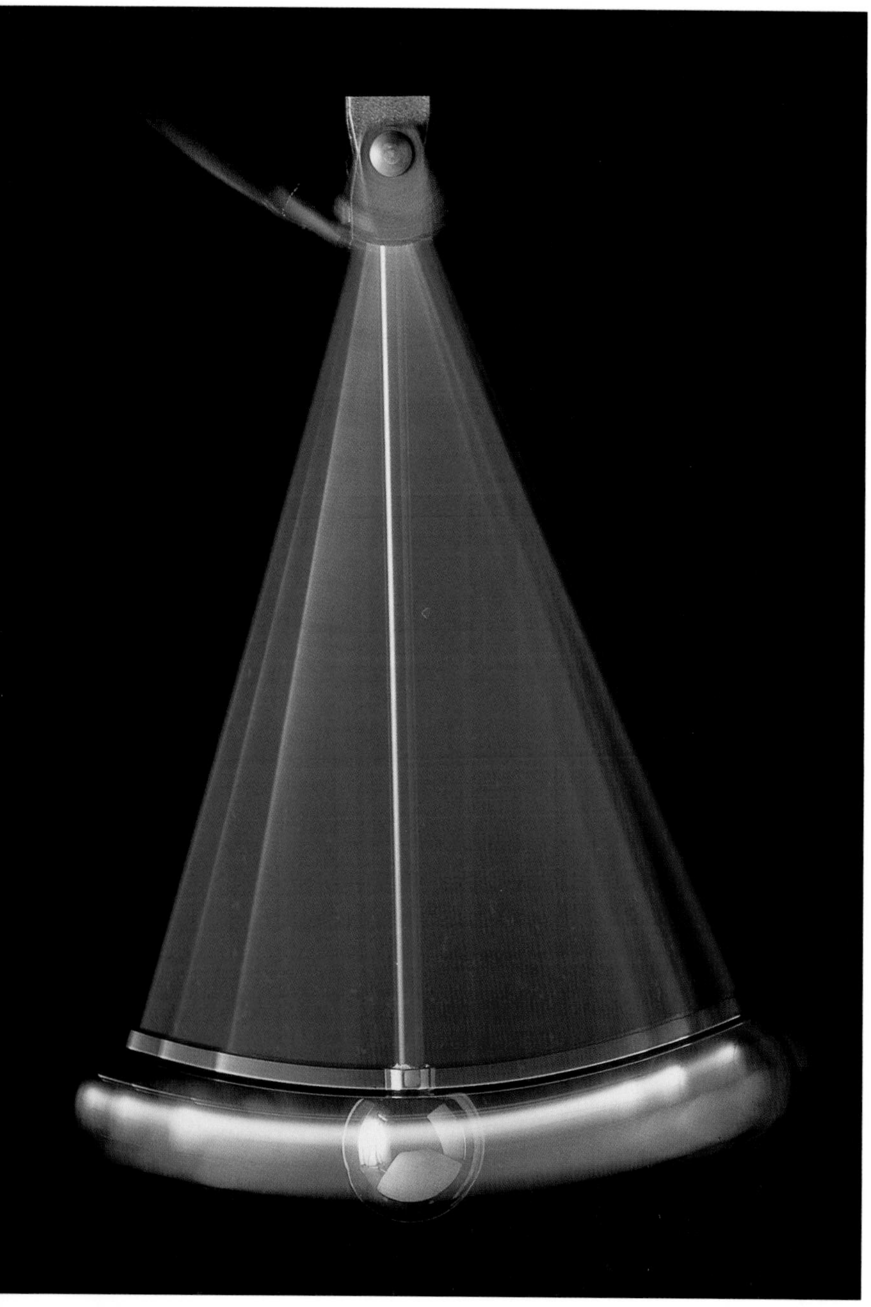

THERE IS A traditional story about the first person to observe the perfectly regular swing of a pendulum—one of many anecdotes told about the Italian scientist Galileo. In 1602, while sitting in the cathedral at Pisa, he noticed the ceiling lamps swinging in the breeze. He did not have a watch (watches had not yet been invented), so he timed the swings using his heartbeat by feeling the pulse in his wrist.

Galileo found that each lamp swung at a regular pace. He also noticed that lamps on long chains swung more slowly than did lamps on short chains. He also wondered whether the heavy lamps swung more slowly than the lighter ones. He could not weigh the lamps, so he did some experiments.

The results of Galileo's experiments with pendulums are illustrated at the top of the opposite page. He found that changing the mass of the bob (the weight at the end of the cord) had no effect on the time of the swing as long as the pendulum swung through only small angles.

◁ **Blurred swing**
The camera was not fast enough to "freeze" the movement of this pendulum. Yet a pendulum *is* momentarily stationary every time it changes direction at the end of each swing.

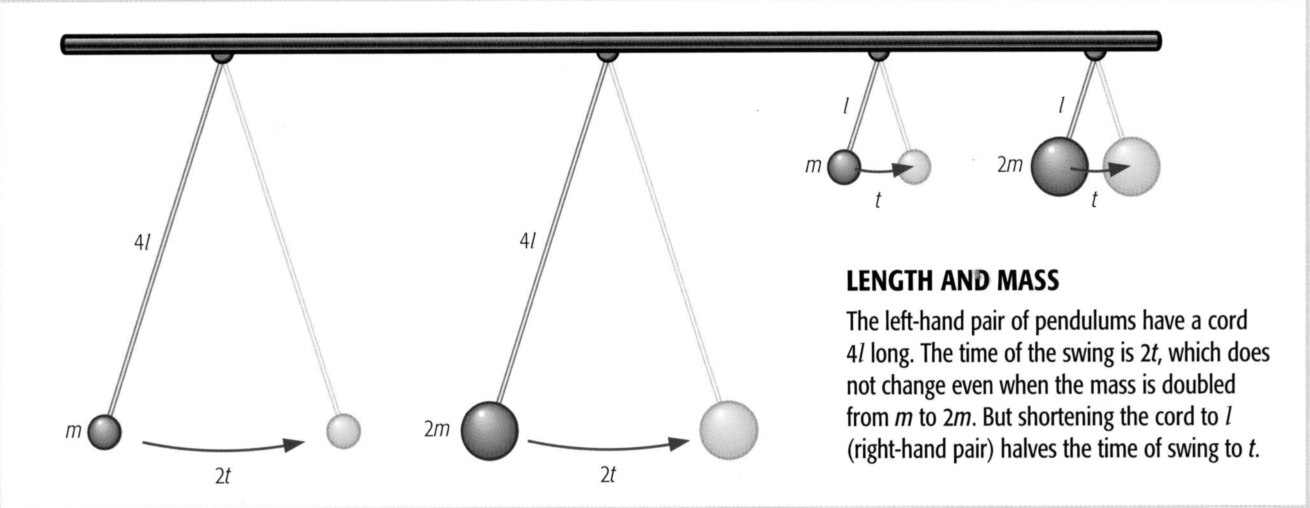

LENGTH AND MASS

The left-hand pair of pendulums have a cord $4l$ long. The time of the swing is $2t$, which does not change even when the mass is doubled from m to $2m$. But shortening the cord to l (right-hand pair) halves the time of swing to t.

But changing the length of the cord did change the time of the swing. This time period was halved when he shortened the cord to one-fourth of its former length.

ENTER GRAVITY

Galileo found that the time for a pendulum's complete swing—that is, from one side, across to the other side, and back again—is proportional to the square root of the pendulum's length. The actual relationship is given by the equation

$$t = 2\pi\sqrt{\frac{l}{g}}$$

where t is the time and l is the length of the cord. Notice that the equation has two other symbols. One is π (pi), which often turns up when circles are involved, and the other symbol is g, the acceleration due to gravity.

USES OF PENDULUMS

The first important application of the pendulum was to regulate the mechanism of a clock. Galileo suggested this, but the Dutch scientist Christiaan Huygens built the first practical pendulum clocks in 1656. The swinging pendulum regulated an escapement, which was a wheel and ratchet arrangement that allowed other wheels to turn slowly, driven by a falling weight or by a spring.

▷ **Primitive clock**
This drawing of part of an early clock shows the pendulum. A single hour hand was attached to the lower spindle–there was no minute hand.

☞ *See also* Force and acceleration **2** : 18; Mass and weight **2** : 10; Motion in a circle **2** : 22

Energy, work, and power

These three things—energy, work, and power—are sometimes confused. Energy is the ability to do work; work results when a force acts over a distance; and power is the rate of doing work. So we will begin with energy, of which there are various kinds.

When asked to do a chore at the end of a tiring day, we may say, "I can't—I don't have the energy." This is a fairly accurate statement, scientifically speaking. Energy is something that, possessed by something else, enables it to do work. As we will see, there are various kinds of energy. We cannot make it or destroy it, which is called the principle of conservation of energy. But we can *use* energy, and in doing so we change it from one of its forms to another form.

The energy we use doing work comes from the food we eat. Food is essentially a mixture of chemicals. The processes of digestion change them into other chemicals, such as the high-energy sugar glucose. When we do work, our muscles use up glucose to provide energy.

KINDS OF ENERGY

Potential energy is energy that something has because of its position. A book on a shelf, for example, has energy stored in it as potential energy. It may look the same as a book on the floor; but if it is knocked off the shelf, the falling book can be made to do work. Imagine tying a string to the book and attaching the other end to a nearby vase. Knock the book off the shelf, and watch it do work on the vase! The water stored in a reservoir behind a dam has potential energy that can do work turning turbines to make electricity.

Strain energy is similar in some ways. When you wind up a clock or pull a bow, you strain the material of the spring or the bow and store energy in it. The clock spring slowly unwinds to work the clock, and the bow very rapidly straightens to speed an arrow to its target.

Kinetic energy is the energy of motion, so it is the form of energy possessed by anything that is moving. A swinging hammer has kinetic energy that can do the work of knocking a nail into a lump of wood. A speeding truck has lots of kinetic energy, which is why it can cause so much damage if it accidentally crashes into something.

Heat and light are also forms of energy. Anything that is hot possesses heat energy that can be made to do work in machines such as steam turbines and automobile engines.

◁ **Potential energy**
The water stored behind the dam represents a huge reserve of potential energy. As the water falls, the potential energy is converted to kinetic energy that can be made to do work by turning turbine blades.

☞ *See also* Heat as energy **3** : 6; Light as a form of energy **4** : 8; Resistance and power **7** : 14

KINDS OF ENERGY

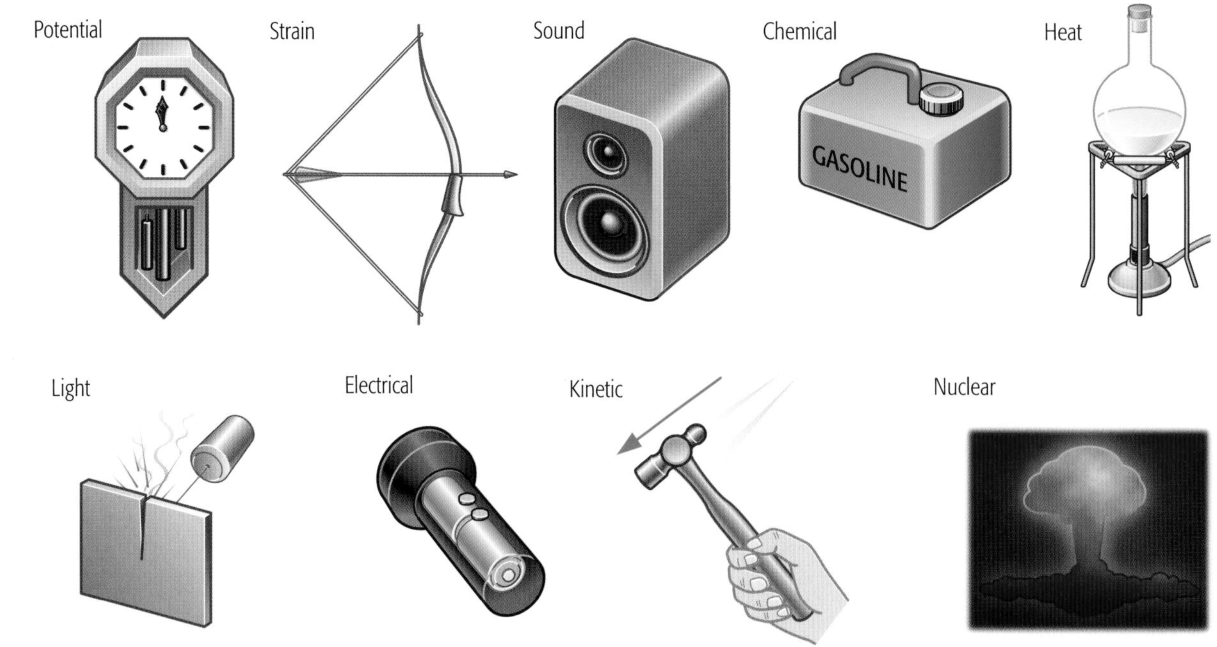

Nine different kinds of energy are illustrated here, from the potential energy of the weights wound up in the clock to the awesome nuclear energy of an exploding atomic bomb, which releases vast quantities of heat, light, and sound.

▷ **Taking the strain**
An archer stretches his bow and takes aim, about to convert the strain energy stored in the bow into the kinetic energy of a speeding arrow.

Green plants use light energy to combine carbon dioxide and water to form sugar and oxygen in the process known as photosynthesis, and light brings about other chemical reactions utilized in photography. The energy of the light in a laser beam is great enough to cut through metal.

Electrical energy is one of the most familiar types of energy. It is produced by batteries and by generators in power plants, and can be made to do all kinds of work from, for example, powering flashlights to driving railroad locomotives.

Sound is a form of energy that is seldom used directly for its energy, although ultrasound is used in medicine and industry to break up kidney stones and cut metals. Prolonged exposure to loud sounds can damage human hearing, sometimes permanently.

The chemical energy locked up in fuels is released when the fuels are burned to produce heat or light. Chemical energy is also released in batteries (but more slowly), where it is converted into electricity.

The final type of energy we need to know about is nuclear energy. It is produced by changes that take place in the nuclei of atoms. Energy is released in fission reactions when large nulcei (such as uranium) split into smaller ones. Nuclear energy also comes from fusion reactions in which light nuclei such as hydrogen nuclei combine to form heavier ones. Fusion reactions take place at the heart of the Sun and other stars, as well as in the hydrogen bomb.

ROLLING BALLS

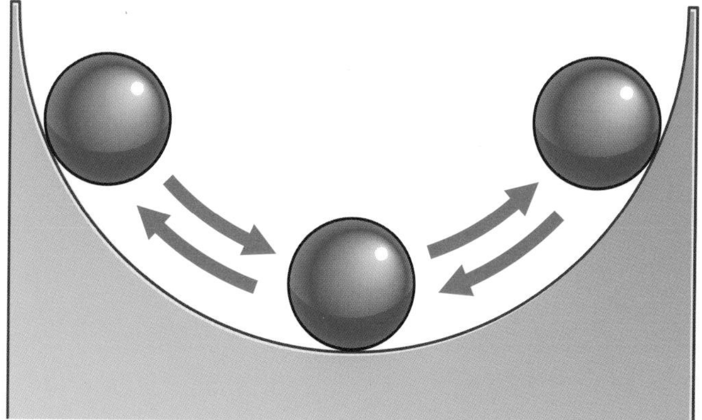

A ball rolling back and forth in a basin switches between having all potential energy (at the highest positions) and all kinetic energy (at the lowest position).

▷ **Roller coaster ride**
Like the ball in the basin at the top of this page, the people on the roller coaster switch between having mostly potential energy to mostly kinetic energy. They do retain some kinetic energy at the top of the ride because they keep moving.

▷ **Chemical catastrophe** The sudden destructive release of chemical energy is evident in this accidental detonation of blasting explosives in a quarry.

INTERCONVERSION OF ENERGY

We noted earlier than energy cannot be created or destroyed, merely changed from one form into another. A few examples should illustrate this point. The pendulum (pages 24–25) is an energy converter. When the pendulum bob is at one end of its swing it has potential energy (because of its position). As it swings across it gains kinetic energy (because it is moving). The potential energy is converted to kinetic energy, which is changed back to potential energy at the other end of the swing.

A speeding bullet also has kinetic energy. When it hits a hard target such as a wall, it stops, and the kinetic energy is converted into heat energy, as well as some sound energy. When a meteorite enters the Earth's atmosphere, friction with the air heats it up (heat energy), and it ionizes atoms in the atmosphere, creating a brief streak of light (light energy), which we see as a falling star.

The food we eat has chemical energy stored in it. This energy drives our body processes, keeps us warm, and is used up in our muscles whenever we do physical work.

ENERGY AND WORK

The energy content of food is generally measured in joules (or calories). And the joule is the unit

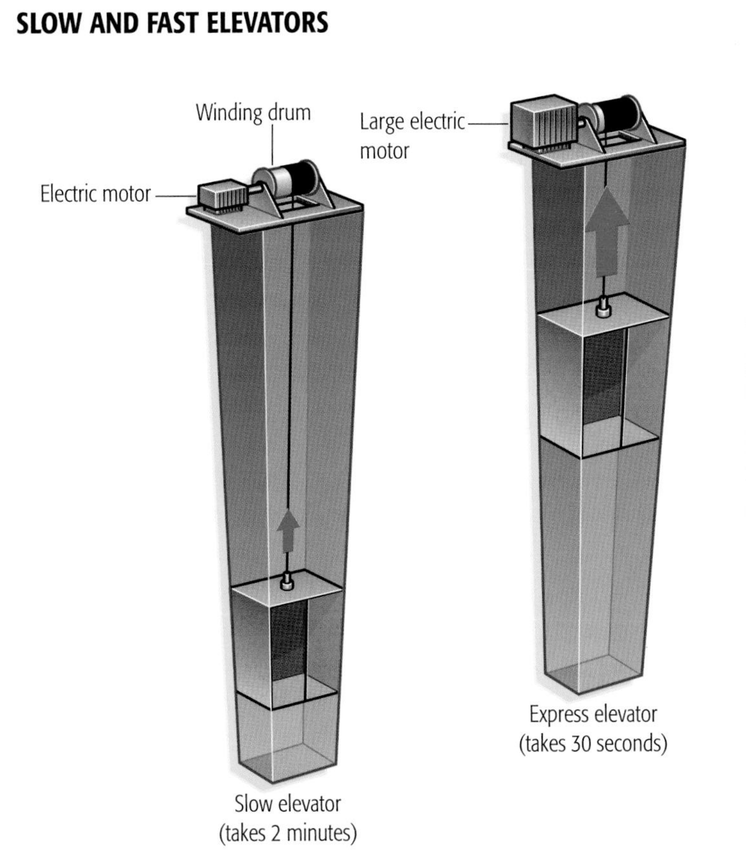

If these two elevators carry the same numbers of passengers, the express elevator needs four times as much power to move four times as fast as the slow elevator. It therefore needs a much larger electric motor to power its winding drum.

used for measuring every other form of energy—for example, heat and mechanical energy. It is possible to compare energy sources in terms of joules. The joule is also the unit for measuring work. In fact, 1 joule is equal to a force of 1 newton moving through a distance of 1 meter. Whenever a force moves something, work is done. For example, if I pick up off the floor a book weighing 20 newtons (i.e., it has a mass of about 2 kg) and place it on a shelf 0.5 m high, the work done by my muscles is $20 \times 0.5 = 10$ joules. If I carry three books up a flight of stairs 4 meters high, the work done is $60 \times 4 = 240$ joules—much more tiring!

WORK AND POWER

Power is the rate of doing work. If I carried those three books upstairs in 12 seconds, the power would be $240 \div 12 = 20$ joules per second. But if I ran up the stairs in just 4 seconds, the power would be $240 \div 4 = 60$ joules per second. (Both of these sums neglect the power that is used in lifting me upstairs.) Although the above calculations give power in joules per second, in physics power has its own unit, the watt (1 watt = 1 joule per second), named after the Scottish engineer James Watt. So in my run upstairs I converted energy at 60 watts—about the same as a dim electric light bulb.

Stability and equilibrium

Normally, when a force acts on an object it makes it move in a straight line in the direction of the force. But in certain circumstances a force may have no effect at all, or cause the object to move in the arc of a circle, or even make it fall over.

▽ **Balanced mobile**
This mobile resembles three seesaws joined together. The top one has another seesaw at one end, which has a third seesaw keeping it balanced.

THE EFFECT OF a force on an object depends on how stable the object is. A cubical box on a table just sits there. It is perfectly stable and shows no tendency to move. If you tilt it slightly, raising one edge off the table, then let it go, it sits back down on the table. In scientific terms it is said to be in stable equilibrium.

A cylinder on its side is slightly different. It will stay where it is put; but if given a slight push, it will roll along. It is in neutral equilibrium. But a narrow cylinder balanced on one end

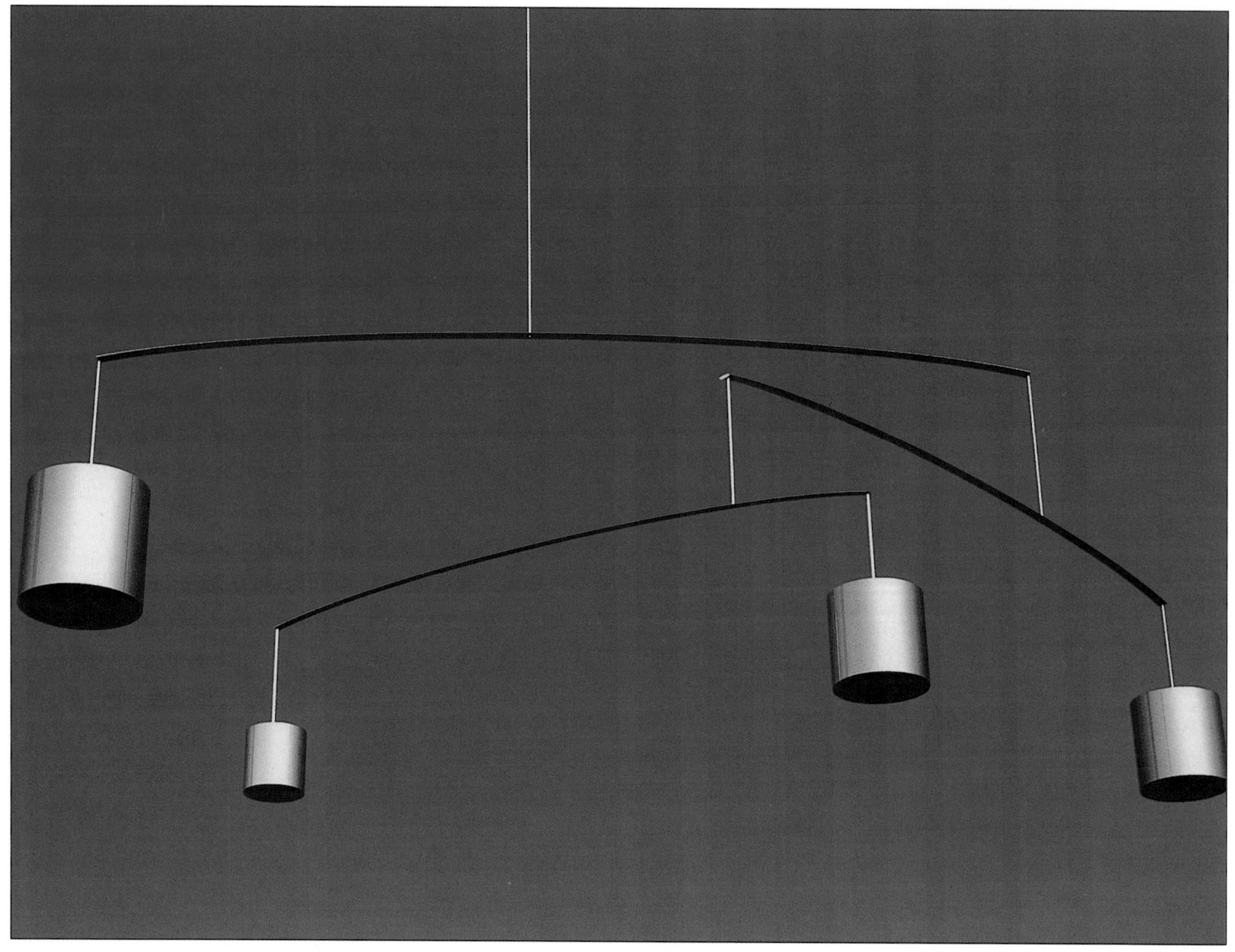

is different. Give it the slightest sideways tilt, and it topples over. It is in unstable equilibrium.

CENTER OF GRAVITY

The point at which all of an object's mass appears to be concentrated is called its center of gravity (also sometimes called center of mass). In the cubical box the center of gravity is right at the center. If you tilt the box, its center of gravity rises slightly. In the cylinder on its side the center of gravity is halfway along its axis (the line joining the centers of each end). When the cylinder rolls, its center of gravity moves sideways but does not move farther up or down.

The same cylinder standing on end has its center of gravity in the same place—halfway along its central axis. But this time, when the cylinder is tilted sideways, the center of gravity moves down slightly, and a vertical line through it meets the table at a position outside the cylinder's base. This combination of circumstances makes the cylinder unstable, and it falls over.

So, the stability of an object depends on what happens to its center of gravity when it is tilted. If the center moves up, the object is in stable equilibrium. If the center moves sideways, it is in neutral equilibrium. But if the center moves down, the object is in unstable equilibrium.

BALANCING FORCES

A seesaw represents a different kind of equilibrium. Think of a seesaw pivoted at its center. It balances on the pivot (which is called a fulcrum in physics)

EQUILIBRIUM

The cube and the cone on its base are both in stable equilibrium, and each falls back onto its base if tilted. The ball and the cone on its side are both in neutral equilibrium and can roll. The cone on its point and the narrow cylinder are both in unstable equilibrium, and they topple if tilted far enough sideways.

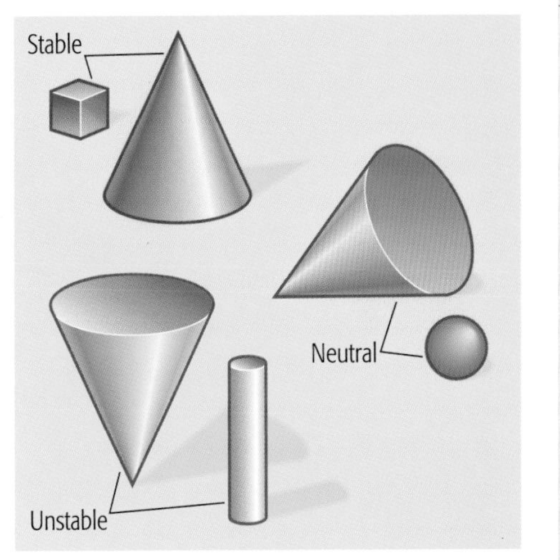

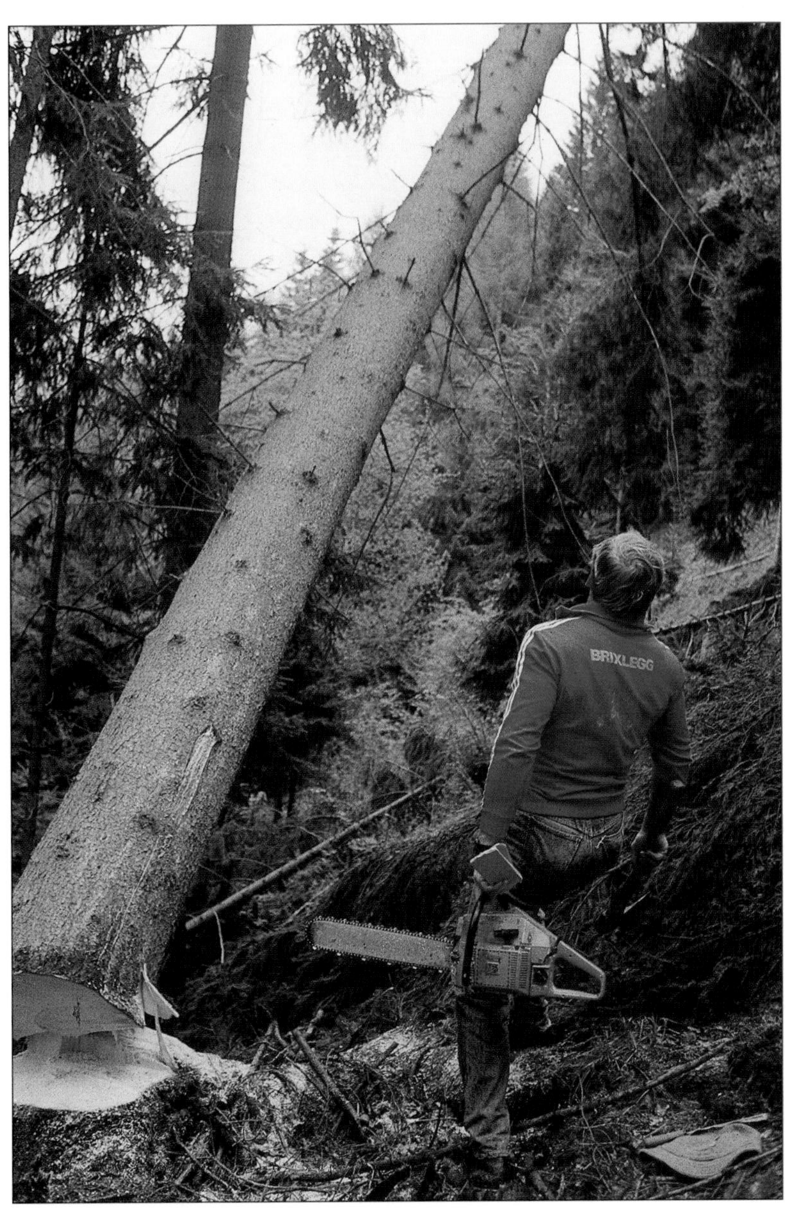

▷ **Tumbling timber**
A tree is stable while it is firmly rooted to the ground. But when it is cut off at the bottom the slightest tilt makes it come crashing down.

☞ *See also* Force and acceleration **2** : 18; Loads and levers **2** : 36; Mass and weight **2** : 10

SIMPLE SEESAW

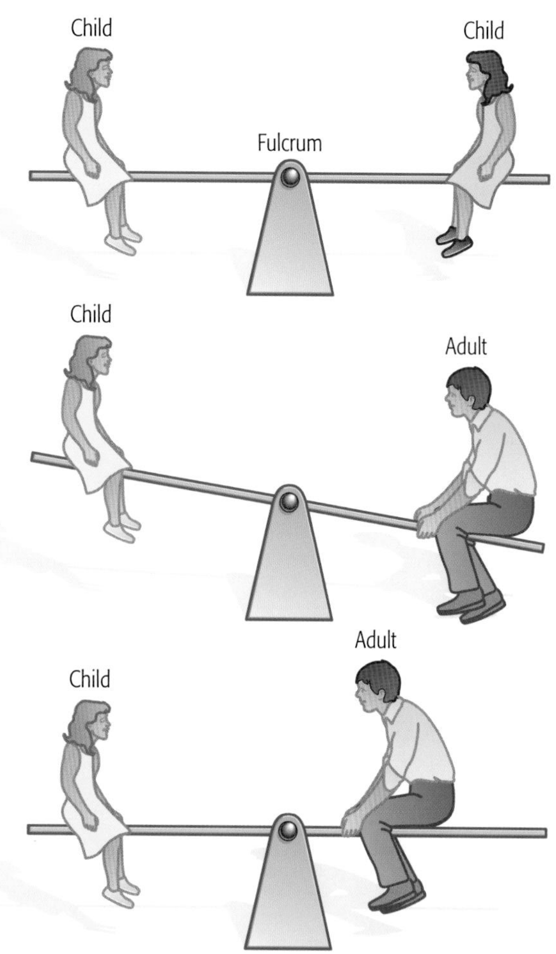

A seesaw is a simple example of turning moments. Children of equal weight balance at equal distances from the pivot. For an adult to have a ride, he or she has to sit closer to the pivot.

because there are equal weights on either side. But add unequal weights to each side—say a child at the end of one side and an adult at the end of the other—and the seesaw tips downward on the heavier side. The unequal forces (the weights of the people are forces) produce a turning effect. This effect is called a turning moment, and its size is equal to the force multiplied by its distance from the fulcrum.

So to balance the seesaw with the child and the adult, we have to make the turning moments the same. The only way to do this is for the adult to move nearer the fulcrum so that the adult's weight multiplied by his distance to the fulcrum is the same as the product of the child's weight and her distance to the fulcrum.

By the way, because a turning moment is equal to a force (measured in newtons, N) multiplied by a distance (measured in meters, m), its units are newton meters, written as Nm. A monkey wrench is a good example of a practical use of turning moments. When changing a wheel on a car with a flat tire, it is not possible to turn the wheel nuts using fingers—they are not strong enough. But using a wrench makes it easy because a force of 100 N applied at right angles to the handle of a wrench 25 cm long produces a turning moment of $100 \times 0.25 = 25$ Nm. The crank between the pedal of a bicycle and the chain wheel acts in a similar way to produce rotation. You also use a turning moment whenever you open a door. It takes more force to open a short wide door than a tall narrow one because the distance from the handle to the hinges is greater.

TWO ARE BETTER THAN ONE

If there are two turning moments acting at the same point, the combined effect of both forces is called a couple.

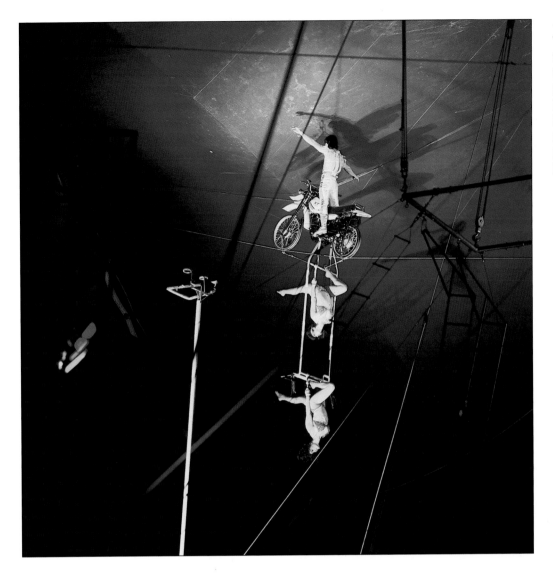

◁ **Not so unstable**
The real balancing act is the man standing up on the motorbike. Because of the weights of the women hanging beneath it, the bike has a center of gravity below the tightrope, and the whole arrangement is stable.

A familiar example is a faucet, which is turned by applying one moment on one side and an equal and opposite moment on the other side. Engineers sometimes use a long cylindrical wrench, called a socket wrench, for undoing stubborn nuts. It has a rod, termed a tommy bar, through one end of the cylinder. The other end goes over the nut, and the engineer applies a turning force to each end of the tommy bar. The turning effect of the couple unscrews the nut. A screwdriver is another example of a tool that uses couples. A screwdriver with a fat handle produces a greater couple and more turning force than one with a thin handle.

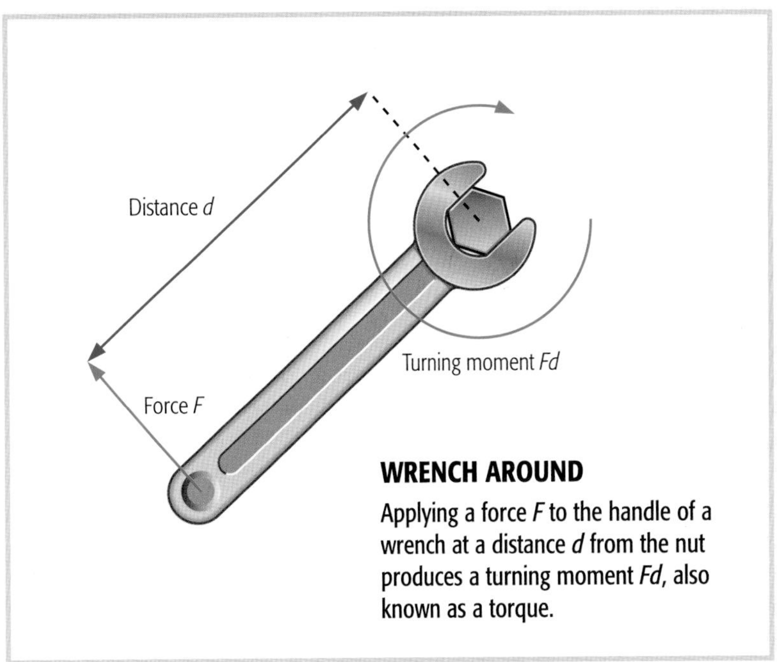

WRENCH AROUND
Applying a force *F* to the handle of a wrench at a distance *d* from the nut produces a turning moment *Fd*, also known as a torque.

Loads and levers

A lever is probably the simplest kind of machine, which we can define as any device that provides a mechanical advantage. But even though they are simple, there are three very different kinds of lever, which have dozens of applications.

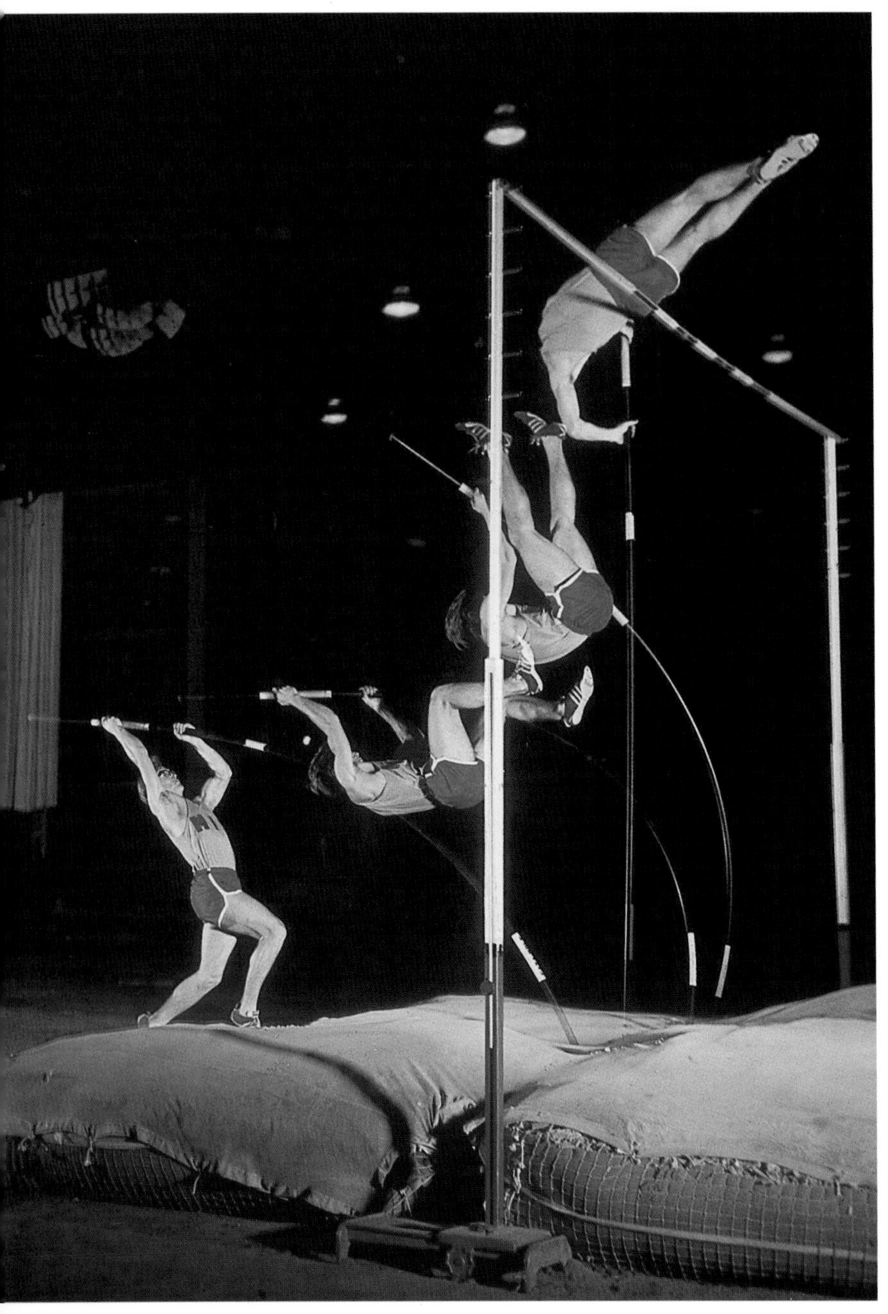

THE GREEK SCIENTIST Archimedes is supposed to have said, "Give me a lever long enough and somewhere to stand, and I will move the Earth." He certainly did make extensive use of levers in the various ingenious machines he designed for his patron, the King of Syracuse.

THREE CLASSES OF LEVER

All kinds of lever have several things in common. They all involve a force, called the effort, that moves a load, making use of a pivot, or fulcrum. Archimedes' Earth-moving lever was a Class 1 lever, which works like a crowbar. Scissors or shears make use of a pair of Class 1 levers. The effort and load act in the same direction on opposite sides of the fulcrum (see the illustration on the opposite page).

In a Class 2 lever the effort and load are on the same side of the fulcrum and act in opposite directions. The load is nearer the fulcrum than the effort. A wheelbarrow is an example of a Class 2 lever.

Finally, a Class 3 lever also has the effort and the load on the same side and acting in opposite directions. But

◁ **Springy lever**
A pole-vaulter's pole acts as a lever to lift him into the air. The vaulter also gets help from the springiness of the pole.

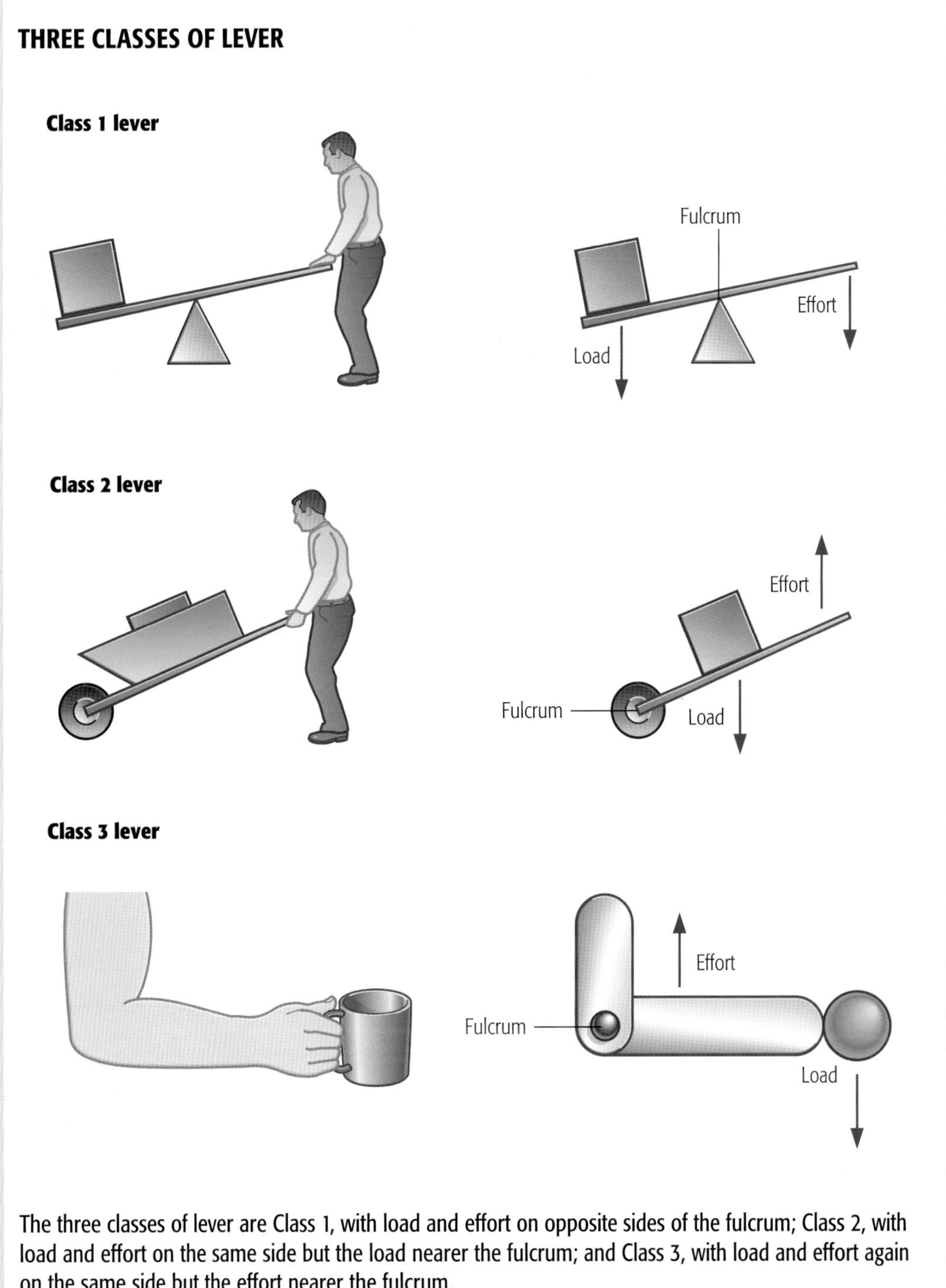

The three classes of lever are Class 1, with load and effort on opposite sides of the fulcrum; Class 2, with load and effort on the same side but the load nearer the fulcrum; and Class 3, with load and effort again on the same side but the effort nearer the fulcrum.

this time the effort is nearer the fulcrum than the load is. The way your forearm works when you pick up something and the way tweezers and tongs work are examples of Class 3 levers in action. In fact, all movements of jointed bones in our bodies involve levers of one type or another.

MECHANICAL ADVANTAGE

In a Class 1 lever, if the distance from the effort to the fulcrum is greater than the distance from the load to the fulcrum, then a small effort can move a large load. We say that the lever provides a mechanical advantage, which is defined as the load (output

☞ *See also* Inclines and friction **2** : 40; Pulleys and gears **2** : 42; Stability and equilibrium **2** : 32

WHEEL AND AXLE

A wheel and axle are used in a windlass for raising a bucket from a well. This can provide a large mechanical advantage.

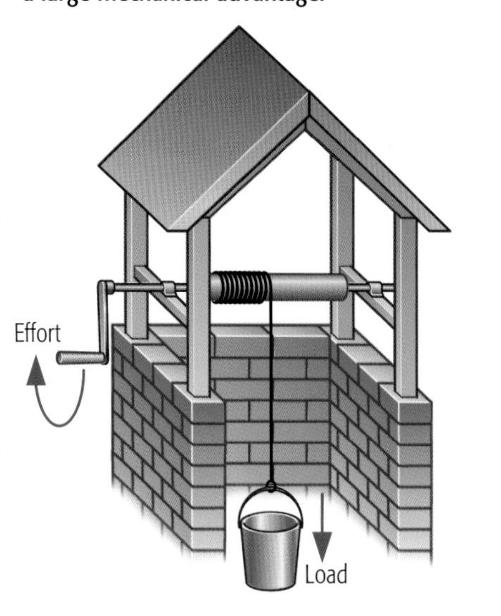

force) divided by the effort (input force). This ratio is also sometimes called the force ratio, and for a Class 1 lever it is equal to the distance from the effort to the fulcrum divided by the distance from the load to the fulcrum. It also equals the distance the effort moves divided by the distance the load moves.

For a lever or any other kind of machine to be useful, the mechanical advantage must be greater than 1. Imagine trying to pry the lid off a tin of paint using a coin as a kind of short crowbar. It acts as a Class 1 lever with a mechanical advantage of about 4. (Because mechanical advantage is a ratio of two forces, it is a pure number and has no units.) If this is not enough to remove the lid, you can greatly increase the mechanical advantage by using a screwdriver to pry off the lid—like a long crowbar. This will provide a mechanical advantage of up to 30, which should be more than enough to open it. The illustrations on these pages show other examples of various levers in action.

DUMP TRUCK

The hydraulic mechanism of this dump truck is an example of a Class 2 lever. Compare it with the wheelbarrow on page 37.

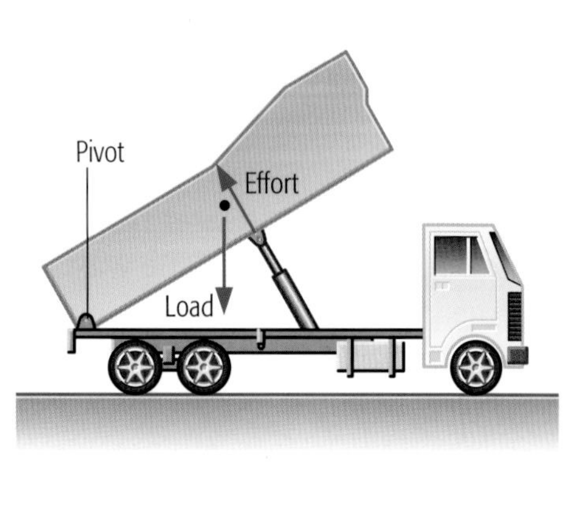

▷ Sharp levers
A pair of garden shears, like scissors, consists of a pair of Class 1 levers working together. The longer the handles, the greater the mechanical advantage.

WHEEL AND AXLE

A windlass is a device that uses a handle to turn a cylindrical drum to wind a bucket up from a well. A capstan used to pull up the anchor chain on a ship is another example. In scientific terms such a device is called a wheel and axle. It is a variety of Class 1 lever in which the effort can be applied continuously.

The input force is applied at the rim of the wheel, and the output force acts at the rim of the axle. If the wheel has a radius of R units and the axle has a radius of r units, the mechanical advantage is R divided by r. A car's steering wheel is another everyday example of a wheel and axle.

MECHANICAL EFFICENCY

All these devices that use levers are examples of simple machines. Some perform better than others—that is, some machines are more efficient than others. Efficiency is the energy (or power) produced by a machine, the useful work done, divided by the energy (or power) it consumes. It is usually expressed as a percentage and is always less than 100 percent since no machine is perfect.

In practice there is usually a difference between any machine's theoretical mechanical advantage and its actual mechanical advantage. The ratio of these two—actual divided by theorectical—is also a measure of efficiency. A simple Class 1 lever is one of the most efficient machines, with an efficiency approaching 100 percent. Other simple machines, such as a screw (see page 41), are extremely inefficient.

LEVERING UPWARD
The cork lifter, or bottle opener, also employs a pair of Class 1 levers. The load is very close to the fulcrum, producing a large mechanical advantage that should shift the most stubborn cork.

Inclines and friction

It is much easier to push a load up a slope than to lift it directly upward. The slope is called an inclined plane, and it is another example of a simple machine that provides a mechanical advantage. Without it the Ancient Egyptians could not have built the pyramids, and screws and bolts would not work.

▽ **Free from friction**
There is very little friction between a skater's skates and the ice. That is because the pressure on the skates (because of the skater's weight) melts the ice slightly and provides a film of lubricating water.

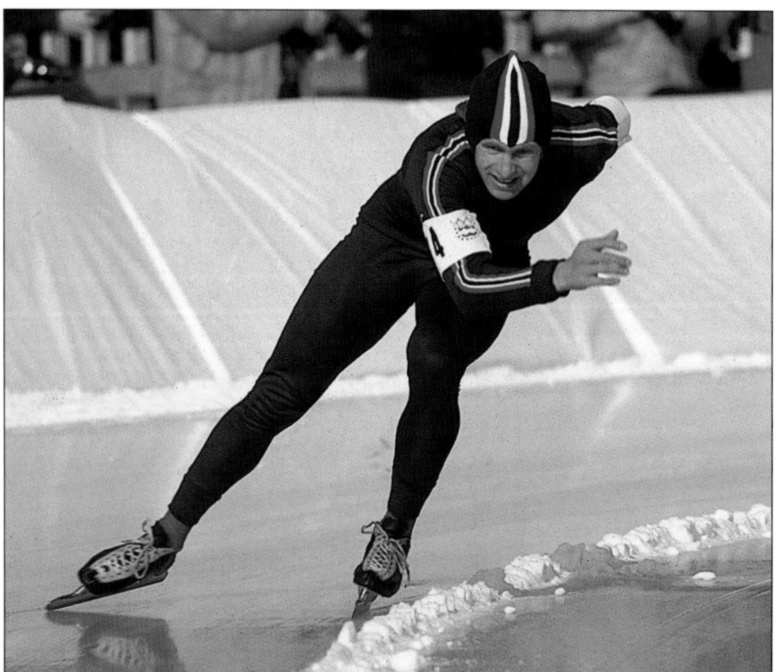

GIVEN THE CHOICE between a steep path straight up a hill or a gentle slope winding upward around it, most people would choose the gentler slope. Similarly, it is easier to climb a set of stairs than a vertical ladder. We do not think of such simple devices as machines, but they are to a physicist. They are examples of an inclined plane.

We have seen that a successful machine provides a mechanical advantage greater than 1. For an inclined plane the mechanical advantage is the load (a downward force) divided by the effort (the force pushing the load up the slope), which is equal to the length of the plane divided by the height of the slope.

A wedge is a simple application of the inclined plane. Imagine driving a wedge under the edge of a heavy block. As the wedge moves in, it gradually lifts the block. This is exactly similar to pushing a block up an inclined plane, and the mechanical advantage is equal to the length of the wedge divided by its maximum thickness. Wedges have many uses, from splitting logs and rocks to forming the cutting part of an ax or chisel. All other cutting tools, from saws to sandpaper, make use of the action of wedges.

It is thought that the Ancient Egyptians built huge earth ramps—inclined planes—spiraling around the pyramids while they were building them. Slaves hauled large blocks of stone weighing many tons up the ramps, probably on rollers to reduce friction between the blocks and the ramp. When the pyramid was finished, after many years of back-breaking work, the ramps were finally dismantled and the earth taken away to reveal the completed structure.

SPIRAL INCLINED PLANES

Winding a wedge (an inclined plane) around a cylinder can create much smaller spiral ramps. The result is a screw thread. When a screw is rotated in a block of wood, its threads cut into the wood and draw in the screw. Screws are tapered, but parallel-sided bolts work in the same way. The long narrow wedge that forms the thread makes a large mechanical advantage. Its value depends on the pitch of the screw, which is the distance it travels forward in one compete rotation. This, in turn, is equal to the distance between the screw's threads.

OVERCOMING FRICTION

A screw remains in a piece of wood because of friction. Friction is a force that tends to prevent stationary objects in contact from moving. Without it a screw would unscrew itself. But in the moving parts of machines friction is a nuisance, representing a waste of energy—for example, it soaks up about half the power of an automobile engine. Oil, grease, and other lubricants between the moving parts reduce friction.

INCLINED PLANE

It is easier to push a load up an inclined plane than to lift it up vertically. The mechanical advantage equals the length of the ramp (*L*) divided by its height (*h*).

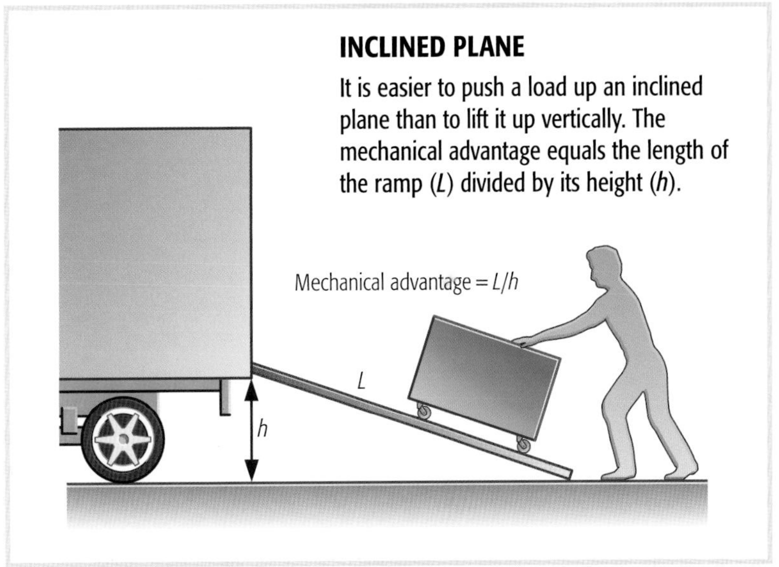

SCREWS AND JACKS

The mechanical advantage of a screw depends on its pitch, the distance between its threads. Rotating a screw enables it to lift things. This is the principle of the jackscrew, as used for lifting an automobile to change a tire.

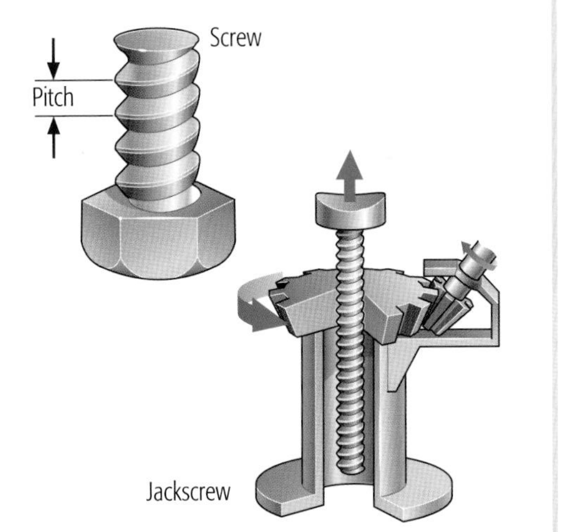

STATIC FRICTION

Static friction–the force needed to start an object sliding along a surface–depends on the object's weight, not on its shape or the area of contact between the object and the surface. All the objects shown here have the same weigh (*W*), and static friction is the same for all of them. Lubricants reduce friction by introducing a layer of softer substance between the object and the surface.

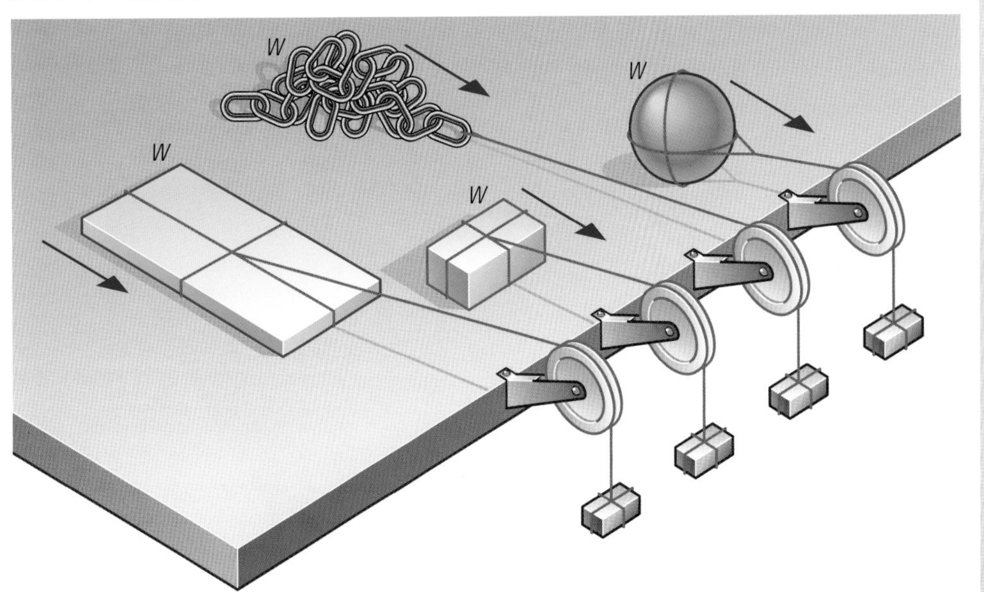

☞ *See also* Energy, work, and power **2** : 26; Loads and levers **2** : 36; Pulleys and gears **2** : 42

Pulleys and gears

Lifting heavy loads was a problem for ancient peoples, whose only help was the inclined plane and, later, the jackscrew. The problem was solved with the invention of pulleys. Later, gears were used to control the output of rotating machinery.

MOST PEOPLE TODAY think of a machine as a useful device with wheels, gears, and other rotating parts. In many ways this idea is correct, although some modern machines (such as an electrical transformer) have no moving parts. We have seen levers and other simple machines on the previous pages, and nearly all of them were devised to help lift a load. One of the best lifting machines is a pulley.

PULLEYS AND PULLING

The simplest pulley has a rope passing over a single grooved wheel, like the type a farmer might use to haul a bale of hay up to the hayloft. In fact, a single pulley is not really a machine at all. Its mechanical advantage (the distance moved by the effort divided by the distance moved by the load) is 1, so there is no real advantage at all. And it cannot be used for lifting anything heavier than the person pulling on the rope. All the single pulley does is to change the direction of a force—the downward pull on the rope lifts up the load.

But with two or more pulleys together the situation is different. Two pulleys give a mechanical advantage of 2, three pulleys give a mechanical advantage of 3, and so on. The number of pulley wheels, or more precisely the number of ropes between them, produces the mechanical advantage of multiple pulleys, usually known as a block and tackle. With three wheels, however, the effort has to move three times as far as the load is lifted. As a result, a lot of rope has to be pulled through the pulley block to raise the load a small distance. Such pulleys came into their own in the days of sailing ships, when they were used to haul up the heavy weight of large canvas sails. They still have many uses today, especially in the large cranes that are used for lifting heavy loads on construction sites and at shipyards.

BELTS AND GEARS

Early sources of power included water wheels and windmills. They needed a way of transferring the rotation of a shaft to other machines, such as millstones for grinding grain. One method was to link a wheel on the driven shaft to a wheel on the other machine using a rope or belt. Ropes ran on grooved wheels (like pulleys), and belts ran over wheels with flat rims. Belt drives were still in use long after the invention of the steam engine for connecting this new source of power to looms and metalworking machinery. The fan belt on a car, which enables the engine to turn the

◁ **Gigantic gears**
On this heavy-duty winding mechanism the smaller gear in front turns faster than the larger gear it drives.

☞ *See also* Energy, work, and power **2** : 26; Inclines and friction **2** : 40; Loads and levers **2** : 36

△ **Lifting heavy loads**
Tower cranes dominate the skyline at a construction site, where their main job is to lift steel girders. All the lifting movements are achieved using pulleys.

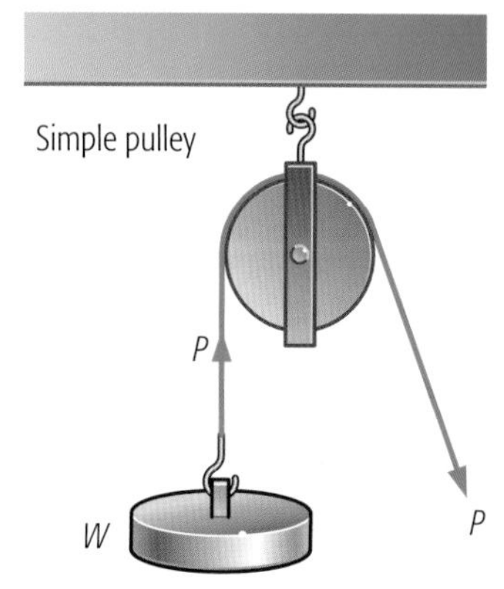

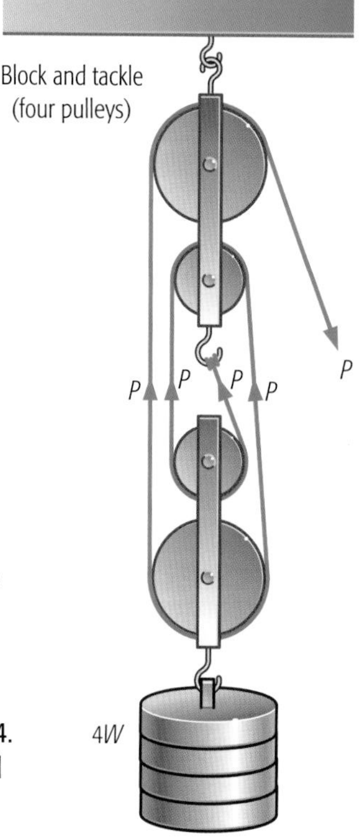

SINGLE AND MULTIPLE PULLEYS

A single pulley only changes the direction of the pull on the rope. A multiple pulley, or block and tackle, provides a mechanical advantage. With four pulleys and four ropes between them the mechanical advantage is 4. The same pull *P* as with the single pulley will lift a load that is four times as heavy.

shaft of the electric generator, is a modern example of a belt drive.

By varying the sizes of the wheels—the drive wheel and the driven wheel—the speed of rotation could be changed. A large drive wheel turns a smaller driven wheel faster, whereas a small drive wheel turns a larger driven wheel slower. Both wheels rotate in the same direction, unless the belt has a half turn like a figure eight.

Larger and smaller wheels were also used when gears began to replace belt drives. Gears, also called cogwheels or cogs, are toothed wheels, usually on parallel shafts, positioned so that the teeth of one engage with the teeth of

DIFFERENT KINDS OF GEAR

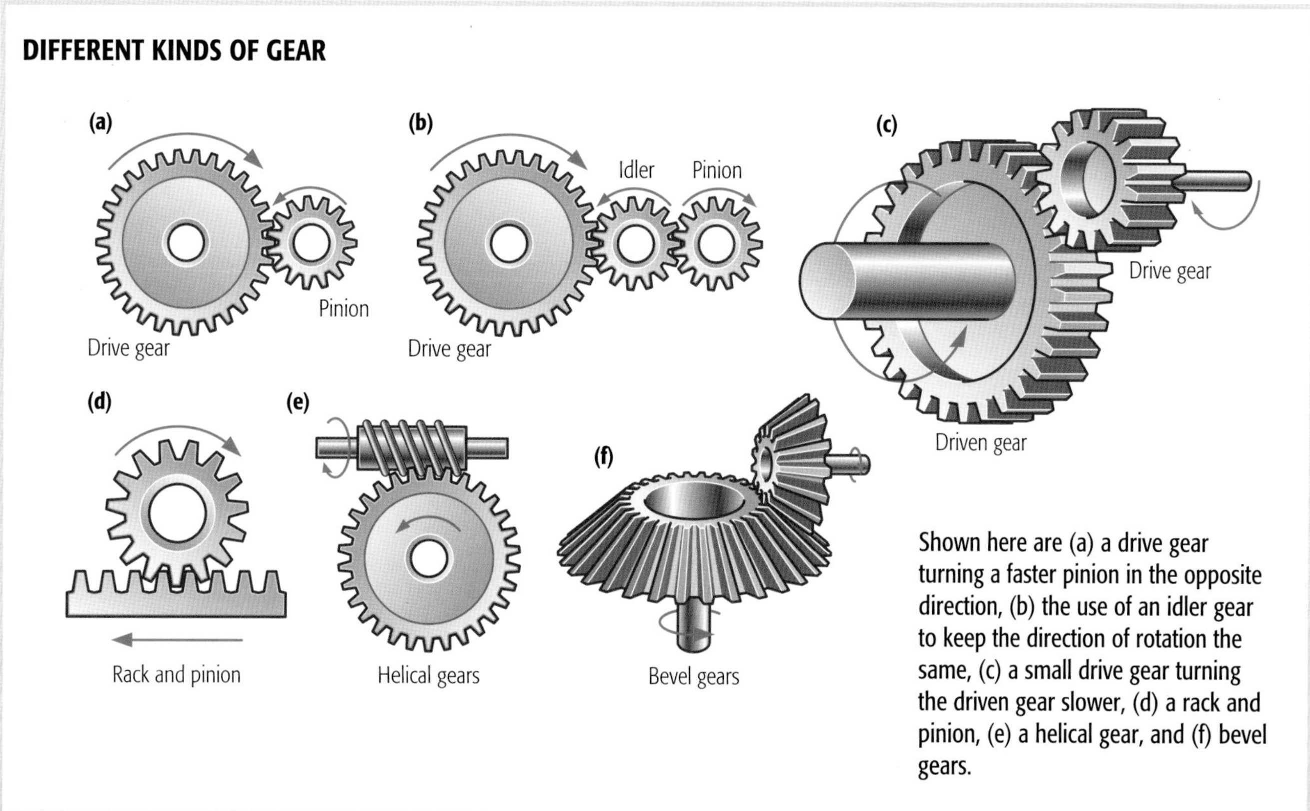

Shown here are (a) a drive gear turning a faster pinion in the opposite direction, (b) the use of an idler gear to keep the direction of rotation the same, (c) a small drive gear turning the driven gear slower, (d) a rack and pinion, (e) a helical gear, and (f) bevel gears.

the other. Again, a large drive gear turns a smaller gear (called a pinion) faster, and a small drive gear turns a larger gear slower. The two gears rotate in opposite directions. To make the pinion gear rotate in the same direction as the drive gear, a free-running idler gear is introduced between the two.

OTHER KINDS OF GEAR

A pinion gear driving a straight rod with teeth cut in it, called a rack, produces a side-to-side movement. It is called a rack and pinion, and is used in the steering mechanism of a car. A gear cut like a screw thread, called a helical gear, can turn another gear on a shaft at right angles to it. Another way of changing the direction of rotation through a right angle is to use bevel gears, which are cut on an angle. (See (d), (e), and (f) in the above illustration for these three different types.)

CROWN WHEEL AND PINION

When a truck or car goes around a curve, the wheel on the outer side of the curve goes farther, and rotates more, than the wheel on the inside of the curve. This arrangement allows it to happen.

❶ Cheating the force of gravity

Whether or not an object can be balanced depends on where its center of gravity is. By setting up objects with unusual centers of gravity, you can seem to cheat the force of gravity.

What you will need

- Two forks
- A flat toothpick
- Modeling clay
- A drinking glass
- A sharp pencil
- A nail file

What to do

Make a small ball of modeling clay and carefully stick in the forks at an angle. Also press the toothpick into the clay, as shown in the illustration. Now balance the whole arrangement on the edge of the drinking glass (you may have to move it slightly back and forth on the edge of the glass to find the best position). It looks like magic!

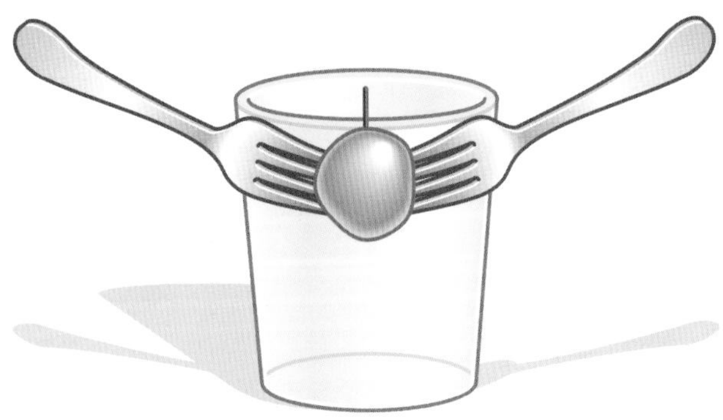

Carefully balance the forks on the rim of the drinking glass.

This "trick" is possible because the center of gravity is in the space between the handles of the forks. As long as the toothpick passes through this point, the whole arrangement will balance with the center of gravity on the edge of the glass.

Another way of showing this is to stick the forks (handles downward) into a lump of modeling clay molded onto a pencil near the pointed end. This arrangement will balance on the point of the pencil–try it on the base of the upturned glass.

If you break off the pencil point and file a notch in the end with a nail file, you can balance it on a tightly stretched length of string, like a tightrope walker.

☞ *See pages 32–35 for more about* ***balance*** *and* ***equilibrium***.

❷ Do heavy things fall faster than light things?

Which falls faster–an iron cannonball or a feather? The famous Italian scientist Galileo was supposed to have tried this experiment by dropping things from the top of the Leaning Tower of Pisa. You can try it with a coin and a piece of paper.

What you will need

- A large coin
- Writing paper
- Scissors

What to do

Cut a disk of paper that is very slightly smaller than the coin. With yours arms stretched out sideways and hands palms down, hold the paper disk horizontally with the fingers of one hand around its edge, and hold the coin the same way in the other hand. Drop them both at the same time. Which hits the ground first?

The paper falls more slowly, but not because it is lighter than the coin. It is slowed down by air resistance and "floats" on the air as it falls. If there were no air, the coin and the paper would fall at the same rate. A NASA astronaut proved this when he was on the surface of the Moon (where there is no air). He dropped a hammer and a feather, and they hit the ground at the same time.

Now try this. Put the paper on top of the coin, and then, holding just the coin by its edges, without touching the paper, drop the two together. This time the paper travels with the coin and hits the ground at the same time. The pressure of air above the coin keeps the paper in place, so that the paper hitches a ride with the coin as it falls.

Try to drop the coin and the paper disk at exactly the same time.

You can repeat the experiment on a larger scale using an old book and a sheet of paper. Cut a rectangle of paper slightly smaller than the book, lay it flat on the book's cover, and drop them both together.

☞ *See pages 10–13 for more about **weight** and **falling objects**.*

❸ The seesaw system

If you and a friend weigh about the same, you can enjoy riding on a seesaw with one of you at each end. But what if an adult wants a ride? How can you balance the extra weight?

What you will need

- Several similar coins (all nickels or all dimes)
- A 30-cm (1-ft) ruler
- A thick pencil

What to do

Place the ruler across the pencil, as shown in the illustration. Put two coins on each end of the ruler, and with the pencil at the center of the ruler, your miniature seesaw will balance. Now carefully put three extra coins on one end of the ruler to make a pile of five coins. These five coins represent the adult, and the two coins at the other end stand for you.

To get the seesaw to balance, you have to move the pencil pivot nearer the end with the five coins. On a real seesaw you would have to ask the adult to sit much nearer the pivot than you (which amounts to the same thing).

On the pencil-and-ruler seesaw note the distance of the two coins to the pencil and the distance of the five coins to the pencil. Multiply the two-coin distance by 2, and multiply the five-coin distance by 5. If you have done your sums correctly, the answers will be the same. Can you think why this is?

☞ *See pages 40–41 for more about **levers** and **pivots**.*

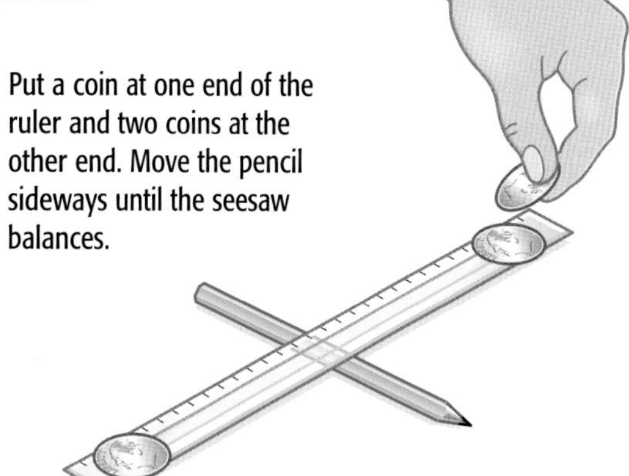

Put a coin at one end of the ruler and two coins at the other end. Move the pencil sideways until the seesaw balances.

4 Check that checker

This project relies on inertia. The idea is to remove the bottom checker from a stack of checkers without touching it or knocking over the stack. As with many such demonstrations, there is a trick to it.

What you will need

- Ten checkers

What to do

Stack nine of the checkers in a neat pile on a shiny surface. Place the tenth checker about 2.5 cm (1 in.) away from the bottom of the stack. With your finger and thumb flick the single checker hard against the base of the stack. The bottom checker will shoot off sideways, leaving the rest of the stack in place. (Some people will find it easier to use the edge of a ruler to flick the bottom checker away.)

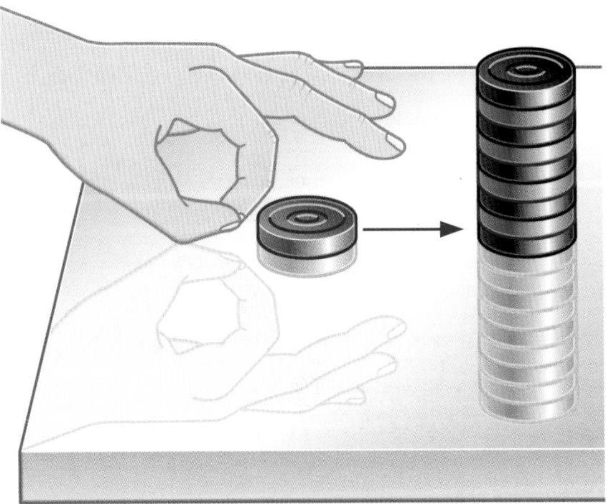

Flick the single checker hard at the base of the pile (or hit it with the edge of a ruler).

Inertia is the reluctance of a stationary object to move. It is inertia that keeps the other checkers from moving even when the bottom one is forced violently sideways. If you master the trick of using a ruler to strike the checker, you can knock out any of the checkers in the stack–not just the bottom one–without disturbing the others.

☞ *See pages 18–21 for more about* ***inertia****.*

5 Car catapult

In Project 4 you proved that stationary objects have inertia. But moving objects also have inertia, which makes it difficult to stop them from moving.

What you will need

- A thick book
- A ruler
- Masking tape
- Modeling clay
- A small free-wheeling toy car
- A pencil
- A table

What to do

Place the book flat on the table, lean the ruler against it to form a ramp, and tape down the lower end of the ruler. Tape down the pencil at right angles to the ruler about two car lengths away. Finally, make a small ball of modeling clay and sit it on the hood of the toy car. Do not press it on too hard, or it will stick–it should be able to fall off easily.

Position the car at the top of the ramp, and let it roll down. It should roll off the end of the ruler until it bumps into the pencil. When it does so, the ball of modeling clay will be catapulted forward. Try making the car go faster by raising the end of the ruler on the book. The faster the car goes, the farther the clay is catapulted. It is the clay's inertia that keeps it moving after the car has stopped.

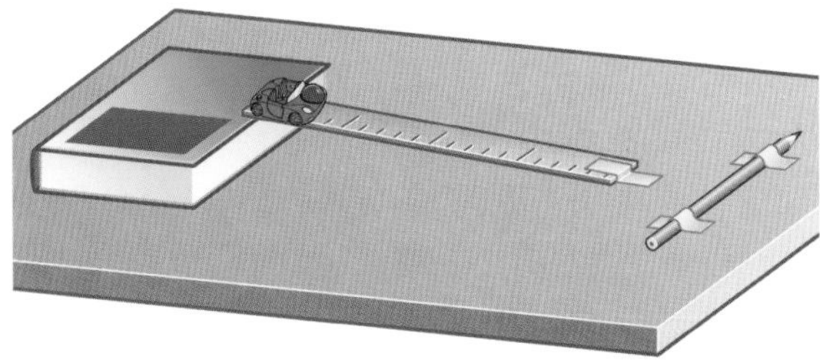

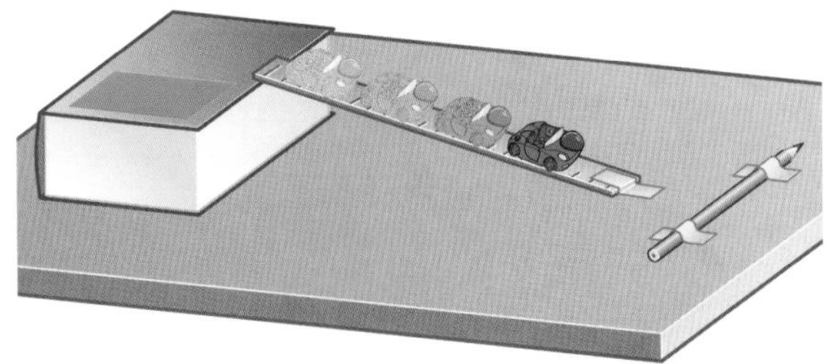

Use a thicker book to make the ramp steeper and the car go faster.

☞ *See pages 18–21 for more about* ***inertia****.*

❻ Rocket balloon

The gases under pressure inside a rocket push in all directions, but the only way they can escape is through the nozzle at the rear of the rocket. A reaction force pushes in the opposite direction, and it is this force that makes the rocket move forward. In this project you use reaction to make a balloon into a rocket.

What you will need

- A long party balloon
- A drinking straw
- Scissors
- Masking tape
- About 3.5 m (12 ft) of string
- Two sturdy chairs

What to do

Cut the drinking straw in half (throw away one half). Thread one end of the string through the straw. Place the chairs about 2.5 m (8 ft) apart, and tie the ends of the string to the chair backs. Move the chairs apart until the string is taut. Cut two short lengths of masking tape, and blow up the balloon. Twist the neck of the balloon to keep in the air. This is where you may need some help. Slide the straw to one end of the string, and tape it onto the inflated balloon. Finally, let go of the neck of the balloon—it will jet along the string under rocket power.

☞ *See pages 18–21 for more about* ***rockets****.*

The escape of compressed air powers the rocket balloon along its string.

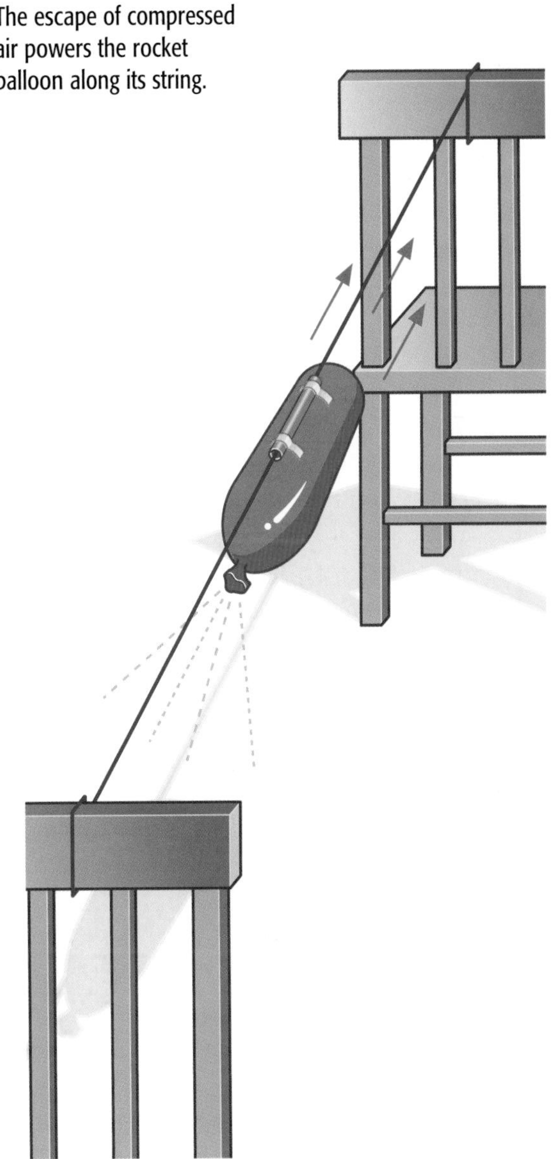

❼ Keep on rolling

Some ancient peoples moved huge heavy objects without any modern equipment. More than 3,000 years ago the Ancient Egyptians built the pyramids from large blocks of stone. They probably dragged the blocks, using hundreds of slaves. To make the blocks move more easily, they probably used rollers. This project uses the Egyptians' methods.

What you will need

- A thick, heavy book
- About 60 cm (2 ft) of string
- A rubber band
- Six round pencils or marker pens
- A table

What to do

Put the book on the table. Make a loose loop of string, and put it around the book, as shown in the illustration, and tie the rubber band to the string. Now pull the book along by the rubber band. The amount the rubber band stretches is a measure of how much force you have to use. Now arrange the pencils or pens as a set of rollers, and put the book on top of them. Pull the book again, and notice how you do not have to use so much force.

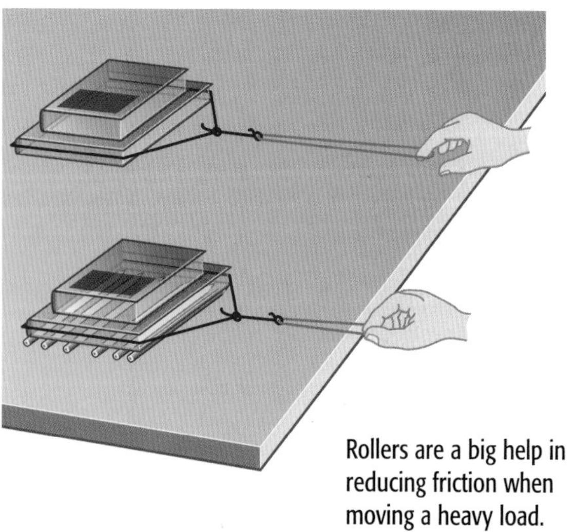

Rollers are a big help in reducing friction when moving a heavy load.

The force you have to overcome to get the book moving is friction. Sliding friction, as between the book and the table, is greater than the rolling friction between the pencils (or pens) and the table. Try placing a second book on top of the first one. Are the two books harder to move?

☞ *See pages 40–41 for more about* ***friction****.*

❽ Spinning water

When objects spin around fast in a circle, there is a force trying to push them in toward the center. It is called centripetal force and is the principle behind a spin drier. The drier makes the wet laundry go around in a circle, but the water moves outward through the holes in the spinning drum, like a hammer thrower's hammer when the athlete lets go of it. This project demonstrates centripetal force.

What you will need

- A large mixing bowl or dish
- A cereal bowl or dessert bowl
- A dish brush
- Water

What to do

Pour water into the large bowl until the water is about 10 cm (4 in.) deep. Float the cereal bowl on the water, and then pour a little water into the cereal bowl until the water is about 1 cm (about $\frac{1}{4}$ in.) deep. Place the brush of the dish brush in the cereal bowl, and use it to spin the cereal bowl around (or use your index finger if you have no dish brush). Keep spinning until the cereal bowl is going really fast.

The water in the spinning bowl will move toward the edge of the bowl and "crawl" up the sides until the bottom of the bowl is dry. As the bowl slows down, the water will sink back toward the center and again cover the bottom. The water has behaved like the water in a spin drier.

Spin the small bowl around and around, and watch the water in it rise.

☞ *See pages 22–23 for more about* ***centripetal force****.*

❾ Swinging low

A weight swinging at the end of a thread or string is called a pendulum. This project looks at what happens if you change the size of the weight, and what happens if you change the length of the thread.

What you will need

- Thread or string
- Various weights, such as a small washer, an eraser, and a small rock
- Two rulers
- Tape
- Scissors
- A heavy book
- A table
- A watch that can time in seconds
- Pencil and paper

What to do

Cut a length of thread to the height of the table above the floor. Place the rulers together, trap the thread between them close to one end of the rulers, and tape the rulers together (at both ends). The idea is to be able to vary the length of the thread by pulling it between the two rulers. Place the rulers so that the thread end overhangs the edge of the table and hold them in place with the heavy book. You can now tie various weights to the lower end of the thread to make pendulums (use tape to attach the rock).

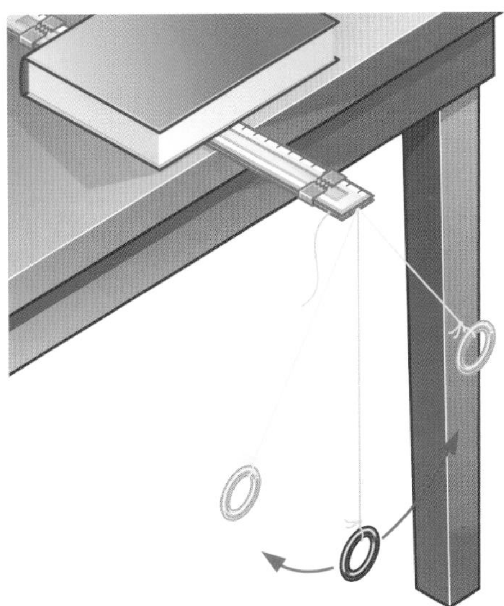

Time the swings with different weights and different lengths of string.

First, try the small washer. Tie it to the thread, pull it to one side, and then let go. Count the number of swings it makes in 10 seconds. It is easier if you have a helper to shout out when 10 seconds are up while you count the swings. Make a note of the answer. Repeat the experiment with heavier weights, and again note how many swings there are in 10 seconds.

Choose another weight, say the eraser, and tie it to the thread. This time vary the length of the thread by pulling it through the rulers, again counting the number of swings in 10 seconds for each length of pendulum. Make a note of your findings.

You should find that the number of swings does not change when you vary the weight at the end of the thread. But the number does vary when you change the length of the thread. In fact, if you shorten the thread to one-fourth of its original length, the pendulum will swing twice as fast.

☞ *See pages 24–25 for more about* ***pendulums****.*

Glossary

Any of the words printed in SMALL CAPITAL LETTERS can be looked up in this Glossary.

Other terms that are explained in an entry are printed in *italic*.

acceleration The rate of change in a moving object's VELOCITY. It is a VECTOR quantity.

acceleration due to gravity Also called acceleration of free fall, the acceleration of any object with MASS falling freely under the Earth's gravity. Its symbol is *g*.

air resistance A FORCE, also called drag or wind resistance, that resists the movement of an object through the air. It is overcome by STREAMLINING.

ampere (A) The SI UNIT of electric current.

balance A device for finding an object's MASS by comparing it with known masses. Devices for finding an object's WEIGHT, perhaps by noting how much it stretches a vertical spring, are also called balances. See also EQUILIBRIUM.

block and tackle A multiple PULLEY, one with two or more pulley wheels.

candela (cd) The SI UNIT of LUMINOUS INTENSITY.

center of gravity Also called center of mass, the point at which an object's total MASS appears to be concentrated and at which it acts.

center of mass Another name for CENTER OF GRAVITY.

centrifugal force A fictitious force sometimes said to act in opposition to (and therefore to balance) the CENTRIPETAL FORCE.

centripetal force The FORCE that acts inward to keep an object moving in a circle.

classes of lever See LEVER.

conservation of energy ENERGY can be neither created nor destroyed, just changed from one form to another.

conservation of momentum In a collision the total MOMENTUM of the objects after impact is the same as it was before impact.

couple The effect of two MOMENTS acting on an object in the same sense (i.e. both clockwise or both counter clockwise) at the same time.

effort In a simple MACHINE the input FORCE (such as that applied to move a LOAD).

energy The capacity to do WORK. There are various kinds, including KINETIC ENERGY, POTENTIAL ENERGY, and STRAIN energy. Heat, light, and sound are also forms of energy. Energy is measured in JOULES.

equilibrium A state of physical balance. If an object in *stable equilibrium* is tilted, its CENTER OF GRAVITY rises, and when released, it falls back to its original position. If an object in *neutral equilibrium* is tilted, its center of gravity neither rises nor falls, and the object merely rolls. If an object in *unstable equilibrium* is tilted, its center of gravity falls, and the object topples over.

fluid A GAS or a LIQUID.

force An influence that changes the shape, position, or movement of an object.

force of gravity Also called gravitation, the FORCE between any two objects arising from their MASSES, most often applied to the force between an object and the Earth (the object's WEIGHT).

force ratio Another name for MECHANICAL ADVANTAGE.

free fall The state of an object that is falling under the Earth's FORCE OF GRAVITY.

friction A FORCE that prevents or slows the movement of one surface against another surface.

fulcrum A pivot, as on a seesaw or where a LEVER pivots.

gas A state of matter in which the molecules move at random and take on the size and shape of their container.

gravitation Another name for the FORCE OF GRAVITY.

hertz (Hz) The derived SI UNIT of frequency.

inclined plane A simple machine consisting of a ramp; the EFFORT is used to push a LOAD up the ramp. A wedge used to split things is also an inclined plane.

inertia The property of an object that makes it tend to resist being moved or, if moving, to resist a change in direction. It is a consequence of the first of NEWTON'S LAWS OF MOTION.

joule (J) The derived SI UNIT of ENERGY equal to the amount of WORK done when a FORCE of 1 NEWTON acts through a distance of 1 meter.

kelvin (K) The SI UNIT of thermodynamic temperature.

kilogram (kg) The SI UNIT of MASS, equal to 1,000 grams.

kinetic energy The ENERGY an object possesses because it is moving.

laws of motion See NEWTON'S LAWS OF MOTION.

lever A simple MACHINE. There are three types or classes: In a *Class 1 lever* the LOAD and EFFORT are on opposite sides of the FULCRUM and act in the same direction. In a *Class 2 lever* the load and effort are on the same side of the fulcrum but act in opposite directions; the load is nearer the fulcrum than is the effort. In a *Class 3 lever* the load and effort are on the same side of the fulcrum and act in the opposite direction; the effort is nearer the fulcrum than is the load.

liquid A state of matter, between a GAS and a SOLID, that has a level surface and, below that surface, takes on the shape of its container.

load In a simple MACHINE the output force (such as that applied by the EFFORT).

luminous intensity The light-emitting power of a source of light.

machine A device that allows one force (the EFFORT) to overcome another (the LOAD).

mass The amount of matter in an object. See also WEIGHT.

mechanical advantage Also called force ratio, in a simple MACHINE it is the LOAD divided by the EFFORT.

meter (m) The SI UNIT of length.

metric system The system of weights and measures, based originally on the METER, from which the system of SI UNITS was developed.

mole (mol) The SI UNIT for quantity of matter.

moment The turning effect (TORQUE) produced when a FORCE acts on an object, equal to the force multiplied by the perpendicular distance of its line of action to the pivot.

momentum The MASS of an object multiplied by its VELOCITY in a straight line.

newton (N) The derived SI UNIT of FORCE. It is the force required to give a mass of 1 kilogram an acceleration of 1 meter per second per second.

Newton's laws of motion Three laws about moving objects: 1. An object at rest will stay at rest, or a moving object will go on moving, unless a FORCE acts on it. 2. The force acting on a moving object is equal to its MASS multiplied by its ACCELERATION. 3. When one object exerts a force on another (the *action*), the second object exerts the same force but in the opposite direction (the *reaction*). In other words, action and reaction are equal and opposite.

potential energy The ENERGY an object possesses because of its position (such as a weight that has been raised to a certain height above the ground).

power The rate of doing WORK or the rate at which ENERGY changes. It is measured in WATTS.

pulley A simple MACHINE consisting of a fixed grooved wheel with a rope running around it. A MECHANICAL ADVANTAGE of more than 1 can be achieved only by using two or more pulleys together.

scalar A quantity that has magnitude but (unlike a VECTOR) no specified direction. Examples of scalars are speed and mass.

second (s) The SI UNIT of time. (The second is also an angular measure, equal to 1/60 of a minute or 1/3,600 of a degree.)

SI units The system of units used internationally in science (short for Système International d'Unités, its name in French). There are seven *base units* (AMPERE, CANDELA, KELVIN, KILOGRAM, METER, MOLE, and SECOND) and various *derived units*, which are combinations of base units.

speed A moving object's rate of change of position (distance traveled divided by time taken). It is a SCALAR quantity (unlike VELOCITY, which is a VECTOR).

standard form A way of expressing very large or very small numbers that uses an index to represent powers of 10. For example, 10,000,000 is 10^7 and 0.000002 is 2×10^{-6}.

strain energy The ENERGY an object possesses because its structure is strained (such as a stretched rubber band).

streamlining The shaping of an object so that it presents the least resistance when moving through a FLUID (gas or liquid).

terminal speed The maximum speed at which an object falls under the influence of gravity.

torque The turning effect of a FORCE on an object. See MOMENT.

triangle of forces A way of adding FORCES using the TRIANGLE OF VECTORS.

triangle of vectors A way of adding VECTORS. The first vector is drawn as a line at the correct angle, with the length of the line representing its magnitude. The second vector is drawn from the end of the first line, again at the correct angle and of the correct length. A third line joining the beginning of the first line to the end of the second line (completing the triangle) gives the magnitude and direction of the sum of the vectors.

vector A quantity that has magnitude and (unlike a SCALAR) direction. Examples of vectors include acceleration and VELOCITY.

velocity A moving object's rate of change of position in a specified direction (distance traveled divided by the time taken). It is a VECTOR quantity (unlike SPEED, which is a SCALAR).

watt (W) The derived SI UNIT of POWER (equal to a rate of working of 1 JOULE per second).

weight The FORCE with which a MASS is attracted toward the Earth (by the FORCE OF GRAVITY).

wheel and axle A simple MACHINE in which a rope is attached to the rim of a wheel, which is fixed to an axle that has another rope wrapped around it. Pulling on the rope to turn the wheel (applying an EFFORT) turns the axle so that its rope will lift a load.

work The ENERGY used when a FORCE moves an object or changes its shape. It is measured in JOULES.

Set Index

Page numbers in *italics* refer to illustrations. Volume numbers are in **bold**. Main entries are in **bold**, with the relevant page numbers underlined. Page numbers in parentheses ( ) indicate that a subject is covered in the activities at the end of the volume. For example:
Electromagnet
making 8: *17,* 24-27, (50) shows that all references are in volume 8, that there is a relevant illustration on page 17, and the main entry is on pages 24 to 27. A project on page 50 is about making electromagnets.

A

Abbe, Ernst **4:** 33
ABS **9:** 34
absolute zero **3:** 11, 45
absorbers, heat 3: 38–41
AC *see* alternating current
acceleration 2: 18–21
circular motion **2:** 22
constant speed **2:** 22
and force 2: 18–21
inclined plane **2:** *11*
Newton's laws **2:** 19
vector **2:** 21
accelerator
linear **10:** 25–26
particle **10:** 24, 25
underground **10:** *27*
accumulator **6:** 42, 44–45
acetylene **1:** 10
acids **6:** 39, **9:** *25, 26*
acoustics **5:** 35
action and reaction **2:** 19–20
balloon rocket **2:** (49)
additive process **4:** 26
Advanced Gas-cooled Reactor **10:** 32
advertising signs **6:** *30,* 32
air 1: 8
compressed **1:** 32, *34, 35*
convection currents **3:** 30–31, 50
drafts **6:** 23–24
expansion **3:** (46–47)
flow **1:** 40, (51)
ionization **6:** 23, *24,* **10:** *23*
lifting **1:** (50)
liquefying **1:** 29
liquid **3:** 45
molecules **6:** 23, *24*
pressure 1: 32–35, (46–47), (50)
thermal conductivity **3:** 29
vibrating columns 5: 16–19, (47)
weight **1:** 8
air bags **1:** (50)
air resistance *see* drag
air-conditioning **3:** 43, **6:** 27
airfoil **1:** 40, *41*
airplanes **1:** 39, 40–41
fly by wire **9:** *43,* 44–45
navigation **2:** *17*
airship **1:** *8,* 10, 21
air-traffic controllers **2:** *16*
alcohol **3:** *11, 19*
alcohol thermometer **3:** 13
ALEPH detector **10:** *26*
alloys **1:** 45
alpha particles **9:** *7,* **10:** 15, 16, *17, 21*
alternating current (AC) 7: 20–21
advantages **7:** 20
DC conversion **9:** 10, *13, 33,* (49)
frequency **7:** 23
generation **7:** 25, *27*
reversal **8:** 35, 40
voltage change **7:** 20–21
alternating current motor *see* electric motor, AC
altimeters **1:** 9
aluminum **1:** 19, 45
anodized **6:** 40
expansion **3:** *25*
extraction **6:** 41
ions **6:** 34
semiconductor impurity **9:** 18, *19,* (51)
thermal conductivity **3:** *28*
aluminum foil **7:** (49)
mirror from **4:** (47)
alveolar sounds **5:** *41*
ammeter **7:** 11, 12, *13*
Ampère, André **8:** 32
ampere (A) **2:** *7,* **7:** 11
amplification
FET **9:** 23
high-power **9:** 13
junction transistor **9:** 22
paper **5:** (51)
radio **9:** (47)
semiconductor **9:** 19, 33
vacuum tube **9:** 10–11
amplitude **5:** 10, *11*
amplitude modulation (AM) **7:** 38
analog signals **7:** 41
anastigmatic lens **4:** 35
aneroid barometer **1:** 9–10
angle of dip **8:** *13*
angle of incidence **4:** 14, 18
angle of reflection **4:** 14
angle of refraction **4:** 18
critical angle **4:** 21
animals
infrasound **5:** 28, 29
navigation **8:** 14, *15*
anion **6:** 34
anode **6:** 31, 32, 33, 38, **9:** *10*
anodizing **6:** 40
ant **9:** *24*
antinode
flute **5:** *19*
pipe **5:** *17,* 18–19
string **5:** *13*
woodwinds **5:** *18*
antiparticle **9:** 15, **10:** 17, 18
Apollo mission **1:** 35, **5:** *32*
apparent depth **4:** (48–49)
Apple II **9:** 36
aqueduct **1:** *42,* 43
Arab clothing **3:** *40*
Arab traders **8:** *6*
arc light **4:** 7
arch **1:** 43–44
archaeology, dating **10:** 21
archer **2:** *28*
Archimedes **1:** 20, **2:** 36
Archimedes' principle **1:** 20, (47)
area
resistance **7:** 15, (51)
thermal conduction **3:** 28
arm
as lever **2:** 37
robotic **9:** *32,* 33
arsenic **9:** 18, *19,* (50)
astigmatism **4:** 35
Aston, Francis **10:** 10, 11
astronomical telescope **4:** 38–39
atmosphere **1:** 36
pollution **6:** *26*
pressure **1:** 8, 9
atmospheric engines **1:** 33
atom 1: 6–7, **10:** *7*
charge **6:** *6,* 34–35, **7:** 6, **10:** *6–7*
chemical reactions **10:** 9
cooling **1:** 28
crystals **1:** 15
electrons **1:** 6, 7, **6:** 6–7, 11, **10:** (47)
hydrogen **6:** 34
images **9:** *6*
ions **6:** 34–35
isotopes **10:** 9–11, (47–48)
magnetism **8:** 7
models **10:** 7, (46)
nucleus **6:** 6, 11
particle accelerator **6:** *21*
relative atomic mass **10:** *10,* 11
scale **9:** (46–47)
solids **1:** 14, 26
stability **9:** 17
structure **9:** 6–7, **10:** 6–7, (46)
theories of structure **9:** 9
versatility **10:** 38–39
vibration **3:** 6, 7, 27
atom bomb **10:** *28,* 29, 31
atom smashers 6: *21,* **8:** 21, **10:** 24–27
atomic clock **2:** *8*
atomic number **10:** 9
atomic pile **10:** *30*
atomic time **2:** *8*
atomic weight *see* relative atomic mass
atto- (prefix) **2:** *9*
attraction
electric currents **8:** *22,* 23
ions **6:** 34
static electricity 6: 8–11, (46–47), (48–49)
see also magnetism
audibility **5:** 36–37, *37*
audible sound range **5:** 26
audiotape **8:** 16, 19
auditory canal **5:** 38, *39*
aurora **8:** *12*
autoclave **1:** 24
automobile *see* car
autopilot **9:** 44

B

bacteria **2:** *6*
bagpipes **5:** *18*
Baird, John Logie **7:** 43
balance **5:** *38,* 39
equilibrium **2:** 33–34
forks **2:** (46)
seesaw **2:** 34, (47)
tightrope **2:** *35*
balances **2:** *8,* 12–13
balloon **1:** 10, 18, 21, **3:** *22,* 23
rocket **2:** (49)
sound conduction **5:** (46)
static electricity **6:** (48–49)
barcode **9:** *44*
Bardeen, John **9:** 18
barium **10:** 28
barometer **1:** 8, 9–10
base units, SI system **2:** *7,* 9
bassoon **5:** 19
bats, ultrasound **5:** 26–27
battery 6: 38, 42–45, **7:** 9, *10*
automobiles **6:** *42,* 44–45
Daniell cell **6:** 44
DC current **7:** *21*
dry **6:** 44
fuel cell **6:** 45
Leclanché cell **6:** 44
mercury oxide **6:** 44
mine tunnel **7:** 10
nickel-cadmium **6:** 44
NIFE **6:** 45
parallel **7:** *11*
polarization **6:** 43–44
primary **6:** 42, 44
secondary **6:** 42
series **7:** *11*
wet **6:** 44
battleship **3:** *20*
bearings, magnetic **8:** 43
beats **4:** 43
Becquerel, A. E. **10:** 16
bel **5:** 32
Bell, Alexander Graham **7:** 34
bell, electric **8:** 28–29
bells **5:** *22,* 23
glass **5:** (49)
spoon **5:** (50–51)
belt drive **2:** 43–44
bent straw illusion **4:** 19
Bernoulli's equation **1:** 39, 40
beryllium **10:** 24, (46)
beta particles **10:** 15–16, *17, 21*
bevel gears **2:** 45
bias
diodes **9:** 21–22
FET **9:** 23
microchip manufacture **9:** 26
semiconductors **9:** *23*
bicycle *see* cycle
Big Bang **10:** *7*
bimetallic strip **3:** 13–14, 24
binary code **9:** 28
binocular microscope **4:** 40
binoculars **4:** 38
biological computers **9:** 45
biological shield **10:** 36, 38–39
biologists **10:** 22–23
bioluminescence **4:** 7
birds, thermal lift **3:** 30, *32*
bits **8:** 18, **9:** 28, 30
black body **3:** 39
black clothing **3:** *40*
black smokers **3:** (49)
blast wave **5:** *8*
blasting **2:** *30–31*
block and tackle **2:** 43, *44*
body, activity measurement **8:** 20
body imaging **8:** 19–20
body temperature **3:** 13
Bohr, Niels **9:** 9, **10:** 7
boiling 1: 22–25, **3:** 18, *19*
boiling-water reactors **10:** 36
bolts **2:** 41
bombs **8:** *23*
bonding
covalent **1:** *7,* 15
intermolecular **1:** 15
ionic **1:** 7, 15, **6:** 34, 36
metallic **1:** 15
solids **1:** 15
boron **9:** 27, **10:** 24, (46)
bottle opener **2:** *39*
Bourdon gauge **1:** *9*
bow **5:** 12
bow and arrow **2:** *28*
Boyle, Robert **1:** 11
Boyle's law **1:** 11
braking **1:** 37, **8:** 43, **9:** 34
brass instruments **5:** 19
Brattain, Walter **9:** 18
breaking point **1:** *44*
breeder reactors **10:** 32–33, 40
brick, thermal conductivity **3:** *28*
bridge **1:** *42,* 43–44, 45
expansion **3:** *24,* 25
Tacoma Narrows **5:** 30
broadcasting
radio 7: 38–41
TV 7: 42–45
brush, electric motor **8:** *35, 36*
bubble chamber **10:** *18*
bubbles **1:** 13, 23
bulbs, Christmas tree **7:** *14*
bulbs, incandescent *see* electric light
bulldozers **1:** 36
bullets **1:** 38–39, **2:** 30
Bunsen burner **1:** 40

buoyancy **1:** 20, 21, (48–49)
burial, dating **10:** *20*
butane **1:** 10
butterfly wing scales **4:** *42,* 43
byte **9:** 28

C

cable laying **7:** *32*
cables **1:** 45
cadmium **10:** 37
calcium **6:** 34
calculators **9:** 41
Calorie **3:** 7
calorie **2:** 30, **3:** 7–8
camera **4:** 36–37
  digital **4:** 37
  lensless **4:** (51)
  pin-hole **4:** (51)
  simple **4:** *36*
  single-lens reflex **4:** *23,* 37
candela (cd) **2:** *7*
CANDU heavy-water reactor **10:** 32
cannon barrel boring **3:** 8–9
capacitor **7:** *12,* 13, **8:** 43
capillary action **1:** 13
car **1:** 34, 36, 37
  battery **6:** 44–45
  cooling system **3:** *32,* 33
  electric **6:** *42,* **7:** 29, **8:** 43
  electric motors **8:** 37
  electromagnetics **8:** 30, *31*
  greenhouse gas **3:** 40
  lightning **6:** 25
  paint sprays **6:** 27, *28*
car body stamping machines **1:** 36
car catapult **2:** (48–49)
carbon **1:** *7,* 15, **10:** 11, (46)
  isotopes **10:** *9,* 11, 19, (48)
carbon dioxide **1:** *7,* 10, 29, **10:** 32, 37–38
  greenhouse effect **3:** 40, *41*
  photosynthesis **4:** 8
  sublimation **3:** 18
carbon fiber **1:** 19, 20, **4:** 7
Carlson, Chester **6:** 28
carnival ride **2:** *22*
carnotite **10:** 40
carrier wave **7:** 38
cathode **6:** 31, 32, 33, 38, **9:** *10*
cathode rays **9:** 8–9
  discovery **9:** 6–7
cathode-ray tube **6:** 16, 31, 32, *33,* **7:** 43, **9:** *11*
  solid state **9:** 12–13
  see also television tube
cation **6:** 34
Cavendish, Henry **2:** *13*
CD **5:** 44–45
CD-ROM **8:** *19,* **9:** 30–31
cellophane, screaming sound **5:** (48–49)
cellphone *see* mobile phone
cells, mobile phone **7:** 40–41
Celsius, Anders **3:** 11
Celsius scale **1:** 26, **3:** 11, 15
  Fahrenheit conversion **3:** 15
  Kelvin conversion **3:** 15
center of curvature **4:** 16
center of gravity **2:** 33
  balancing forks **2:** (46)
  and stability **2:** 33, *35*
center of mass *see* center of gravity
centi- (prefix) **2:** 7, *9*
centigrade *see* Celsius scale
centrifugal separation **10:** 13
centripetal force **2:** *23,* (50–51)
ceramic insulator **6:** 19
CERN **8:** 21, **10:** 26, 27
CFCs (chlorofluorocarbons) **3:** 43
chain reaction **10:** *30*
change of state *see* latent heat
charge *see* electric charge
charging by contact **6:** 12–13
Charles, Jacques **1:** 29
Charles' law **1:** 29, **3:** 22
checkers, inertia experiment **2:** (48)
chemical energy **2:** *28,* 29, *30*
  explosives **2:** *30–31*
  heat **3:** 8
chemical reactions
  atoms **10:** 9
  bonding **1:** *7*
  electrons **10:** 9
Chernobyl disaster **10:** 34, *35*
Chicago Fair Exhibitiion **6:** 21
chimes **8:** *29*
chiming spoon **5:** (50–51)
chloride ion **6:** 34
chlorine **1:** 7, **6:** 34, *35, 38,* **10:** 11
chlorofluorocarbons (CFCs) **3:** 43
Christmas tree bulbs **7:** *14*
chromatic aberration **4:** *32*
chromium plating **6:** 40, *41*
church bells **5:** (50–51)
circuit **7:** *30*
  current flow **7:** 9–10
  series/parallel **7:** 15, *16,* (50)
circuit board **9:** *27*
circuit breaker **7:** 30
circuit etching **9:** 26
circular motion **2:** <u>22–23</u>
clarinet **5:** 19
cleaning, ultrasound **5:** 27
clinical thermometer **3:** 13
clock **9:** 41
  office building **8:** *39*
  pendulum **2:** 25
  water **2:** *8*
cloud chamber **10:** 18
clouds **1:** *25, 31*
  formation **3:** *30,* 31
  lightning **6:** 22, 23, *24, 25*
coal **10:** 37, 38
cobalt, magnetic **8:** 11
cochlea **5:** 38, *39*
cochlear implant **5:** 39
Cockcroft, John **10:** 24, *25*
coefficient of linear expansion **3:** 25
cogs (cogwheels) **2:** *42,* 44–45
coil
  loudspeaker **8:** 30
  magnetic field pattern **8:** 22–23
  magnetic force on **8:** *33*
  see also electromagnet; solenoid
coiled coil flament **7:** *19*
cold light **4:** 7
colliders **6:** *21,* **8:** 21, **10:** 26–27
color
  fluorescent tubes **6:** 32
  and heat **3:** 35–36
  heat radiation **3:** 39–40
  and light **4:** <u>24–29</u>
  white light **4:** (47)
color printing **4:** 27–28
color transparency **4:** 40
color wheel **4:** (47)
colored fringes **4:** 43, *44,* (49)
colored light
  differential focus **4:** *32*
  mixing **4:** 25–27
  primary **4:** 26
  secondary **4:** 26
colored pigments
  mixing **4:** 27–28
  primary **4:** 27
  secondary **4:** 27
column of air, vibrating **5:** <u>16–19,</u> (47)
comb, static electricity **6:** 7, 9, 26, (46–47), **7:** 6, 9
combustion **3:** *9*
Commodore PET **9:** 36
communications *see* telecommunications
communications satellites *see* satellite communications
compact disk **5:** 44–45
compass **8:** 7, 12, *14,* (49)
composite materials **1:** 19–20
compound microscope **4:** *40*
compounds **1:** 6
  salts **6:** 35
compressed air, sound conduction **5:** (46)
compression **1:** 32–33, 44
compression waves **5:** 8, *9*
compressor **1:** 32–33, *34,* 35
  refrigeration **3:** *44*
computer, PC **9:** <u>36–39</u>
  business **9:** 38–39
  home **9:** 36–37
  palmtop **9:** *37,* 39
  peripherals **9:** 37–38
  portable **9:** *37,* 39
  quantum **9:** 45
  storage **8:** 18–19, **9:** <u>28–31</u>
computer networks **9:** *38*
computer-aided design (CAD) **9:** 38–39
comsat *see* satellite communications
concave lens **4:** 31
concave mirror **4:** 15–16
  image **4:** 16–17
  magnification **4:** 17
concert flute **5:** *19*
concert hall, acoustics **5:** 35
concrete **1:** 44, **3:** *10*
condensation **1:** 28, **3:** 18, *43*
condenser (atmospheric) **1:** *31*
condenser (light)
  microscope **4:** 40
  new/old **6:** *17*
  projector **4:** 40, *41*
  storing charge **6:** 17
condenser (refrigeration) **3:** 42, *44*
conduction *see* conduction *under* heat; electrical conduction
conductivity, thermal *see* thermal conductivity
conservation of charge **6:** 11
consonants **5:** 41
construction industry **1:** 43, 45
container testing, radioactivity **10:** *40*
containment buildings **10:** *34, 36,* 37
continental drift **8:** 15
control room, recording studio **5:** *45*
control systems **9:** 33, 34–35
convection currents **3:** 30–31, 50
convection of heat **3:** 30–33, <u>30–33,</u> *37*
  forced **3:** 33
  gases **3:** 30–31, (50)
  liquid **3:** 31, 33, (49)
  oceans **3:** 33
  vacuum bottle **3:** 40
  water **3:** 30, *32,* 33
convex lens **4:** 30, *31*
convex mirror **4:** 16, 17
Cooke, William **7:** 32
cooling **1:** <u>28–31,</u> **3:** <u>42–45,</u> (51)
  atoms **1:** 28
  car **3:** *32,* 33
  crystals **1:** 31
  evaporation **1:** 24–25
  gases **1:** 28–29
  liquids **1:** 30, (49)
  liquids/gases expansion **3:** 42, *44*
  metals **1:** 31
  molecules **1:** 28
  nuclear reactors **10:** 31, *32, 33, 34,* 36
  solids **1:** 15, 30
cooling towers **1:** *28,* **7:** 23, *24*
copper **1:** 6, 15
  expansion **3:** *25*
  ions **6:** 39, (49–50)
  purified by electrolysis **6:** 41
  specific heat capacity **3:** *17*
  thermal conductivity **3:** *28*
copper oxide **1:** 6
copper plating **6:** 41
copper sulfate **6:** 39
cork **3:** 29
cork, thermal conductivity **3:** *28*
cork lifter **2:** *39*
corn **4:** *8*
corrosion, resistance **6:** 40
corrugated iron, painted **4:** *24*
cosmic rays **10:** 15
Coulomb, Charles **6:** 10
Coulomb's law **6:** 10–11
couples **2:** 34–35
covalent bonding **1:** *7,* 15
crane **2:** *44*
  electric motor **8:** *34*
  electromagnetic **7:** 28, **8:** 21, *24*
crank **2:** 34
Cray supercomputer **9:** *33*
critical angle **4:** 21
critical temperature **3:** 43
Crookes, William **7:** 43, **9:** 6, 9
Crookes tube **9:** *8, 9,* 14
crowbar **2:** 36, 38
crown and pinion **2:** 45
cruise control **8:** 30
crust, Earth **5:** 31
cryogenics **3:** 45
crystals **1:** <u>14–17</u>
  artificial **9:** *16*
  atoms **1:** 15
  axes **1:** *17*
  cooling **1:** 31
  diamond **1:** *7*
  gallium arsenide **9:** *17*
  halite **6:** *34*
  hardness **1:** 45
  internal structure **6:** 11
  ionic **6:** 11, *35*
  ions **1:** 15
  lattice **1:** 14, 16, 17
  metal **1:** 6, 7, *7,* 15
  molecules **1:** 15
  particles **1:** 15
  resistance **7:** 18
  salt **6:** 34, *35*
  silicon **9:** *16*
  snow **1:** 30, **3:** *43*
  solids **1:** 14, 15, 30, **6:** 36
  as thermometer **3:** *13*
  unit cells **1:** 17
  x-rays **1:** 17
cumulus clouds **3:** *31*
Curie, Marie **10:** 16, *19*
Curie, Pierre **10:** 16
current *see* alternating current; direct current; electric current
curved mirror **4:** 15–17
customs, x-rays **9:** *14*
cutting tools, as wedges **2:** 40
cyan **4:** 26
cycle crank **2:** 34
cycle dynamo **7:** *26*

cycle pump **1:** *34*
cyclist, tightrope **5:** *38*
cyclotron **10:** 24–25
cylinder **1:** 33–34, 37
  phonograph **5:** 42
cymbals **5:** *22,* 23

D

dam **1:** *14,* 39, **2:** *26,* 27
Daniell, John **6:** 44
Daniell cell **6:** 44
data compression, HDTV **7:** 45
data storage **8:** 18–19, **9:** 28–31
Davy, Humphry, arc light **4:** 7
DC *see* direct current
De Forest, Lee **9:** 13
deafness **5:** 39, 41
deca- (prefix) **2:** *9*
deci- (prefix) **2:** *9*
decibel (dB) **5:** 32–33
deflection plates **6:** 32, *33*
degaussing **8:** 26
demagnetization **8:** 16, 26
density **1:** 18–21, (48–49)
  aluminum **1:** 19
  ice **1:** 18–19, 30
  liquids **1:** 12
  mass **1:** 18
  refraction **4:** 18
  sound transmission **5:** 11, (46)
  steel **1:** 21
  volume **1:** 18
  water **1:** 18–19, 30
  wood **1:** 18
depolarizer **6:** 44
depth, apparent **4:** 19–20
depth illusion **4:** 18–19
derived units **2:** *7*
desert islands illusion **4:** *20*
detection, electric charge **6:** 12–15, (48–49)
detector, radio **9:** (47)
detergents **1:** 13, **6:** 27
deuterium
  fusion **10:** *43,* (51)
  heavy water **10:** 31, (49–50)
  neutrons **10:** 9
  tokamak **10:** 45
  Urey, H. **10:** 12–13
Dewar, James **3:** *39*
Dewar flask **3:** 39–40
dhow **8:** *6*
diamond **1:** *7,* 15, 16
dielectric **6:** 17, **7:** 13
Diesel, Rudolf **1:** 34–35
diesel engines **1:** 34
differential gear **2:** *45*
digestion **2:** 27
diggers **1:** 36, *37*
digital camera **4:** 37
digital signals **7:** 41
digital thermometer **3:** *12*
diode
  biasing **9:** 21–22
  current flow **9:** *22*
  light-emitting **9:** *20*
  rectification **9:** 10, *13,* 22, (49)
  solid-state **9:** 20–22
  tube **9:** 10, *13*
dip **8:** *13*
direct current (DC) **7:** 20, 20–21
  from AC **9:** 10, *13,* *33,* (49)
  generation **7:** 25–26, *27*
  motor **8:** 34–35, *36*
disk, phonograph **5:** 42
disks, computer **8:** 18, **9:** 29–30
dispersion **4:** 23, 29
displacement **1:** 20, 21, (47)
distance **2:** 6
  gravitational attraction **2:** 13
distance estimation **5:** 34
distortion of sound **7:** 39
dog whistles **5:** 26
dolphins **8:** *14–15*
domains *see* magnetic domains
domestic appliances **7:** *17,* 31, **8:** 37
domestic heating, solar panels **4:** 9
door chimes **8:** *29*
doping **9:** 17–19, (50)
Doppler, Christian **5:** 25
Doppler effect **5:** *25*
drafts, air **6:** 23–24
drag **1:** 40–41, **2:** 14–15, (46–47)
drag racing **2:** *20–21,* **3:** *8*
DRAM **9:** 29
drawing waves **9:** (48–49)
drinking glasses, bells **5:** (49)
driving mirror **4:** 17
drums **5:** *20,* 21, *22,* 23
ductility **1:** 15, 45
dump truck, lever mechanism **2:** *38*
dust removal, electrostatic **6:** 26–27
DVD **8:** *19,* **9:** 31
dynamic RAM **9:** 29
dynamo **7:** *26*

E

ear, human **5:** 38–39
ear protectors **5:** *33*
earpiece, telephone **7:** 34, *35*
Earth
  geographic poles **8:** 12, *13*
  magnetic field **8:** (49)
  magnetism **8:** 12–15
  shadow **4:** 10–11
  structure **5:** 31
Earth-Moon forces **2:** 19
earthquake **5:** *28,* 30–31
ebonite **6:** 20, *22*
ECG (electrocardiograph) **9:** *12*
echo **5:** 34–35
echo location **5:** *27*
eclipse **4:** 10–11
Edison, Thomas Alva **4:** 7, **5:** 42, **6:** 45
efficiency, mechanical **2:** 39
effort, levers **2:** 36–37
Einstein, Albert **10:** 25–26, 27, 28–29, 42
elasticity **1:** 44–45
elastomers **1:** 44
electric battery *see* battery
electric bell **8:** 28–29
electric car **6:** *42,* **7:** 29, **8:** 43
electric charge **1:** 6–7, **6:** 6–7
  advertising signs **6:** *30,* 32
  atom **6:** *6,* 34–35, **10:** *6–7*
  attraction **6:** 8–11
  carrier **6:** *21, 22,* **9:** 17–19
  conductors **6:** 14, 37, 39, 50
  conservation of charge principle **6:** 11
  contact charging **6:** 12–13
  detection **6:** 12–15, (48–49)
  distribution **6:** 14–15, 16, *17*
  electric field **10:** 10
  electrons **6:** 6–7, 11, **10:** *6*
  force **6:** 10–11
  friction **6:** 7, 8, 11, 14
  induction **6:** *12,* 13, 15, 20
  insulators **6:** 14
  ions **6:** 38, (50)
  magnetic fields **10:** 10
  moving electrons **6:** 30–33, **7:** 6–7
  negative/positive **6:** 6, 7, 8
  neutralization **6:** 15
  nucleus **10:** *7*
  particles **6:** 31
  pointed objects **6:** 15
  production **6:** 18–21
  repulsion **6:** 8–11
  separation **6:** *24*
  storing **6:** 17, *21,* **7:** *12,* 13
  testing **6:** *13,* 14
  thermionic emission **6:** 31, *32,* **9:** 10
  see also static electricity
electric current **7:** 6–7, **9:** 8–9
  effects **7:** 7
  flow direction **8:** 22
  generation **7:** 9
  heating **7:** 7, *7,* **9:** 8–9
  magnetism **7:** 7, **8:** 23, *33*
  measurement **7:** 12–13
  nature of **9:** 8–9
  Ohm's law **7:** 14–15
  power **7:** 18
  resistance **7:** (51)
  series/parallel resistances **7:** 15, *16*
  stored charge **7:** 12–13
  unit **7:** 11
  vacuum tube **9:** 10
electric discharge, lightning **6:** 22
electric energy **2:** *28,* 29
electric field **6:** 16–17
  charged particles **10:** 10
  electromagnetism **8:** 1, *17,* 20–21
  metal container **6:** *19*
  shape **6:** 16, *17*
electric furnace **7:** 28
electric guitar **5:** *14,* **8:** 31
electric heater **7:** (49)
electric light **4:** *6,* 7, **7:** 16, 18–19, (47)
  electron movement **9:** 8–9
  filaments **1:** 23, 26
  inert gases **7:** 19
  switch **7:** *30*
electric motor **8:** 34–37
  car **8:** 37
  crane **8:** *34*
  DC **8:** 34–35, *36*
  domestic machines **8:** 37
  and industrialization **8:** 39
  motor effect **8:** 32–33
  pithead **8:** *38*
  stopping/starting **8:** 40–41
  two-pole **8:** 40
  uses **8:** 38–41
electric motor, AC **8:** 35–36
  elevator **8:** 39–40
  induction **8:** 36–37, *40*
  linear induction **8:** 37, 40
  rotation direction **8:** 41
  speed control **8:** 41
  synchronous **8:** 41
electric potential, cloud **6:** *24*
electric power transmission **7:** 23–24
electric telegraph *see* telegraphy
electric vehicles **8:** 42–45
electrical conduction
  acid **6:** 39
  lightning **6:** 15, 24–25
  liquids **6:** 37
  metals **1:** 15, 31, 45, **7:** *7,* 9, (46)
  potato **6:** (49–50)
  testing **6:** 14, **7:** (46)
  water **6:** (50)
electricity
  domestic **7:** 30–31
  heat from **3:** 8, *9*
  magnetism **8:** 22–23
  at work **7:** 28–29
  see also static electricity
electricity generation **6:** 19, 20–21, 45, **7:** 9, 22–27
  deregulated **7:** 27
  electrostatic **6:** 19, 20
  environmental impact **7:** 23
  "green" **7:** 27
  nuclear power **10:** *37*
  radioisotope thermoelectric **10:** 39
  rotary **6:** 19–20
  solar **4:** 8–9, **9:** *42*
  Van de Graaff **6:** 20–21
electricity supply
  distribution **7:** 23–24, *24–25*
  domestic **7:** 30
  meter **7:** 16–17
  safety **7:** 31
electrocardiograph (ECG) **9:** *12*
electrodes **6:** 38, 39
electroforming **6:** 41
electrolysis **6:** 38–39, **10:** (50)
  chlorine **6:** *38*
  gases **6:** 39
  metals **6:** 41
  uses **6:** 40–41, (51)
  water **10:** 13
electrolyte **6:** *36,* 37–38, 39
electromagnet
  AC motor **8:** 35–36
  colliders **8:** 21
  current source **8:** 24–25
  early example **8:** *27*
  field direction **8:** *25*
  Henry's apparatus **8:** *25*
  lifting **8:** 20–21
  loudspeaker **8:** 30, 31, *31*
  magnetization by **8:** 16, *17*
  making **8:** *17,* 24–27, (50)
  microphone **8:** 31
  principles **8:** *25*
  recording **5:** 43–44
  relay **8:** 29–30
  saturation **8:** 24
  soft **8:** 24, *25*
  solenoids **8:** 24
  strength **8:** 24, (51)
  superconducting **3:** 45
  telephone **7:** 34
  testing **8:** (51)
  uses **8:** 20–21
  see also coil; induction
electromagnetic devices **8:** 28–31
electromagnetic radiation **7:** 36, **10:** 14, 15
  see also gamma rays; x-rays
electromagnetic separation **10:** 13
electromagnetic waves **3:** 35, *36–37*
  see also wave type (e.g. x-rays)
electromotive force (e.m.f.) **7:** 10–11
electron **1:** 6–7, 15, **6:** *23,* **7:** 6, **10:** *7*
  atom **6:** 6–7, 11, **10:** (47)
  beam **6:** 32, *33*
  charge **6:** 6–7, 11, 31, **9:** 17–19, **10:** *6*
  chemical reactions **10:** 9
  conduction **3:** 27–28
  discovery **9:** 6–7
  energy levels (shells) **9:** 17
  gamma rays **9:** 15
  mass **9:** 8
  movement **6:** 30–33, **10:** (47)
  neutron emission **10:** 18
  positrons **9:** 15, **10:** *26*
  pressure **9:** *9*
  properties **9:** 8–9
  quantized orbitals **9:** 9
  scale **9:** (46–47)
  semiconductors **9:** 16–17
  shells **9:** 17
electron beam
  deflection **9:** *11*
  electron microscope **8:** *26,* 27
  see also cathode-ray tube; television tube

electron flow **7:** 6–7
n-type semiconductor **9:** (50)
p-type semiconductors **9:** (51)
semiconductors **9:** 18–19, 21–22
transistor control **9:** 22
triode **9:** 11
vacuum tube **9:** 10
x-ray production **9:** 14
electron micrograph **9:** *6*
electron microscope **1:** *6*, **8:** *26*, 27
electron orbitals **9:** *7*, 14, 17
electronic memory 9: 28–31
electronic music **9:** 45
electronic trading **9:** *40*
electronics, impact on society 9: 40–45
electrophorus **6:** 20, *22*
electroplating **6:** 40–41, (51)
electroscope **6:** 12–15
electrostatics *see* static electricity
elements **1:** 6
elephants, infrasound **5:** 29
elevator **2:** *31*, **8:** 39–40
e-mail **9:** 38, 42
embedded circuits **9:** 33, 34–35
e.m.f. *see* electromotive force
endoscope **4:** 21
energy 2: 27–31
electrical **7:** 16
forms **2:** 27–29, *30*
heat as 3: 6–7
interconversion **2:** *29*, 30
light as 4: 8–9
sound intensity **5:** 32–33
superconductivity **7:** 17
units **2:** 30–31 (*see also* joule)
energy consumption **7:** *17*
energy sources **10:** 31, 37–38, 42, 44
alternative **7:** 26–27
food **2:** 27, 30
sunlight **4:** 8–9
see also **nuclear energy**
energy transfer, heat **3:** 6–7
engine control **9:** 34–35
engine wear **10:** 22
epiglottis **5:** 40, *41*
equilibrium 2: 32–33, 32–35, *35*, (46)
esophagus **5:** 40, *41*
etching, circuit manufacture **9:** *25*, *26*
ethane **1:** 10
ether **1:** 23
Etna, Mount **1:** *26*
evaporation 1: 22–25, **3:** 18
cooling **3:** 42, *44*, (51)
exa- (prefix) **2:** *9*
expansion 1: 11, 30
air **3:** (46–47)
apparent **3:** 21
cooling **3:** 42, *44*
fluids 3: 20–23
gases **3:** 22–23
ice **3:** 21, (48)
liquids **3:** 20–22
solids 3: 24–25
water **3:** 21–22, (47)
expansion joints **3:** *24*, *25*
expansivity **3:** 25
gases **3:** 22–23
liquids **3:** 20–22
solids **3:** 21, 25
explosion, blast wave **5:** *8*
explosives **1:** 35
extraction of metals **6:** 41, (51)
eye, human 4: 34–35
eyepiece **4:** 38, *40*

F

Fahrenheit, Gabriel **3:** 11
Fahrenheit scale **3:** 11, 15
Celsius conversion **3:** 15
Kelvin conversion **3:** 15
fair weather clouds **3:** *31*
falling objects 2: 14–15
fan belt **2:** 43–44
fan motor **8:** *40*
Faraday, Michael **6:** 15, **7:** 23, **8:** 27, 32–33
faucet, couples **2:** 35
fax (facsimile) **7:** 33
feathers **3:** *28*
feedback control **2:** *23*
feet, heat detectors **3:** (51)
femto- (prefix) **2:** *9*
Fermi, Enrico **10:** 30, 31
fermium **10:** 31
ferrites **8:** 11
fetus **5:** *27*
fiber optics **4:** 21
fiberglass **1:** 19, 20
field, magnetic *see* magnetic field
field magnets **8:** 35–36
field-effect transistor (FET) **9:** *21*, *22*, 23
filament **4:** 7, **7:** 18, 19, (47)
fipple **5:** 17
fire fighting **1:** 10, *12*, *36*
firedamp **3:** *28*
firefly **4:** *7*
fireworks **1:** 35, **5:** *6–7*
fish **3:** 21–22, **4:** 7
fishing, sonar **5:** *34–35*
fission *see* nuclear fission
fixed points **3:** 10–11
Fizeau method, speed of light **4:** 12–13
flame, as light **4:** 6–7
flashlights **6:** 44
flicker, TV **7:** *44*, 45
floating 1: 18–21, (48–49), (50–51)
floppy disk **8:** 18, *19*, **9:** 29–30
flow
fluids **1:** 38–41, (51)
gases **1:** 11
flower growing **3:** 41
flowerpot cooler **3:** (51)
flue pipes **5:** 17
fluids
expansion 3: 20–23
flow 1: 38–41, (51)
see also convection; gas; liquid
fluorescent tube **4:** *6*, **6:** 32, *33*
fluorine **10:** 9, 13, (46)
flute **5:** *19*
fly by wire **9:** *43*, 44–45
flywheel **8:** 43
FM (frequency modulation) **7:** 38–39
foam plastics **3:** 29
focal length **4:** 16, *31*
focus
curved mirror **4:** 16
defects **4:** 35
lenses **4:** 30, 31
sharp **4:** 33
focusing, light
camera **4:** 37
human eye **4:** 34
projector **4:** 40
focusing, sound **5:** *10*
fog warning **5:** *36*
food, energy source **2:** 27, 30
force 2: 18–21, **6:** 10
and acceleration 2: 18–21
electric charge **6:** 10–11
electric field **6:** *16*
and motion **2:** 18
as vector **6:** 10
force ratio *see* mechanical advantage
forearm
as lever **2:** 37
measuring instrument **2:** *8*
forks, balancing **2:** (46)
Franklin, Benjamin **1:** 23, **6:** *23*
free electrons **9:** 16–17
free fall **2:** 15
freeze-drying **3:** 18
freezing **1:** 30–31
freezing point **1:** (49)
French horn **5:** 19
freon **3:** 42, 43
frequency **5:** 10, *11*
apparent **5:** 25
fundamental **5:** 13, *15*, *17*, 18
human perception **5:** 38
speech **5:** 41
string length **5:** 13
string tension **5:** 13
string weight **5:** 14
frequency modulation (FM) **7:** 38–39
frets, guitar **5:** 13, *15*
friction 1: 38, **2:** 18–19, 40–41, **6:** *7*
charge **6:** 7, 8, 11, 12, 14
heat **3:** *8*, 8–9, 9
rollers **2:** (50)
static **2:** *41*
static electricity **6:** 31
superfluidity **3:** 45
fringes **4:** 43, *44*
Frisch, Otto **10:** 28, 29
fuel **1:** 10, 29, **2:** 29, **6:** 26–27
fuel cell **6:** 45, **7:** 29
fulcrum **2:** 33–34, 36, *37*
functional MRI **8:** 20
fundamental frequency **5:** 13, *15*, *17*, 18
fur insulation **3:** *29*
furnace **3:** *26*, **4:** *14*
fuse **7:** 30
fusebox **7:** 30
fusion *see* nuclear fusion
fusion (heat) **3:** 18

G

g (acceleration due to gravity) **2:** 15, 25
Galilean telescope **4:** 38
Galileo Galilei **2:** 12
acceleration due to gravity **2:** 11, 14
acceleration on inclined plane **2:** *11*
Leaning Tower of Pisa **2:** 14
pendulum **2:** 24–25
gallium arsenide **9:** *17*
gallons, unit differences **2:** *7*
galvanometer **7:** 13
gamma rays **3:** *36*, **9:** 15, **10:** 14, 15–16, *17*, *21*
gas 1: 32–35
compressed **1:** 32–33
convection **3:** 30–31, (50)
cooling **1:** 28–29
critical temperature **3:** 43
electrolysis **6:** 39
elements **1:** 6
expansion **1:** 11, **3:** 22–23
flow **1:** 11
fuels **1:** 10, 29
molecules **1:** 36
oil refinery **1:** 10
particles **1:** 8
pressure **1:** 8, 10–11, 28, 32–35
propellant **1:** 35
properties **1:** 10–11
temperature **1:** 11, 29
vapor **1:** 23
volume **1:** 11, **3:** 22
water **6:** 39
see also fluids
gas, liquid **1:** 29, **3:** 43, 45
hydrogen **10:** 18
nitrogen **3:** *11*
pressure **3:** 43
vacuum bottle **3:** 39–40
gas control valve **3:** 25
gas fuel **10:** *23*, 38
gas lighting **4:** 7
gas-turbine engine **1:** 35
gas volume, absolute temperature **3:** 22
gas-diffusion separation plant **10:** 13
gears 2: *42*, 42–45, 44–45
belt drive **2:** 44
cogs **2:** 44–45
pulleys 2: 42–45
Geiger counter **10:** *14*, *15*, *23*
gemstones **1:** *15*, 16
generators *see* electricity generation
geostationary orbit **7:** 40–41
geothermal energy **3:** 9
germanium **9:** *19*, (50), (51)
geyser **1:** *22*
giddiness **5:** 39
giga- (prefix) **2:** *9*
Gilbert, William **8:** 14
girders **1:** 44
glass **1:** 14, 30, **3:** *17*, *28*
glass bells **5:** (49)
glass harmonica **5:** (49)
glass wool **3:** *28*, *29*
glassblower **3:** *26*
gliders, thermal lift **3:** 30
Global Positioning System (GPS) **9:** 43–44
global TV **7:** *42*
global warming **3:** 40, *41*, **10:** 38
gold **1:** 15, 19, 20, **3:** *17*
gold plating **6:** 40
gongs **5:** 23
Goodyear airship **1:** *8*
gourds **5:** 20, 21
governor **2:** *23*
GPS (Global Positioning System) **9:** 43–44
granite **10:** 15
graphite **1:** *7*, **10:** 30–31, *32*, *34*
grass fire **3:** *6–7*
gravitational attraction
distance **2:** 13
Saturn's rings **2:** *23*
gravitational constant **2:** *13*
gravity **2:** 11, **6:** 10
acceleration **2:** *11*, 14
bending light **2:** *12*
free fall **2:** 15
g **2:** 15, 25
law **2:** 13
orbiting bodies **2:** 22–23
pendulum swing **2:** 25
spacecraft acceleration **2:** 19
terminal speed **2:** 14–15
Great Eastern (ship) **7:** *32*
greenhouse effect **3:** 40, *41*
greenhouse gases **10:** 37–38
grid **9:** *10*, 11
ground wire **7:** 31
guitar **5:** 13, *14*, *15*, **8:** 31
gun
ear protectors **5:** *33*
gas expansion **3:** *20*, 23
gunpowder **1:** 35
gypsum **1:** *16*

H

hair cells (cochlea) **5:** 38
hair standing on end **6:** *6*, 7, *25*
hair-drier **8:** *40*
half-life **10:** 20, (48–49)
halite **1:** 16, **6:** *34*
Haloid Company **6:** 28
hammer thrower **2:** *23*
hammering, magnetization by **8:** 16, *17*
handoff **7:** 40

hard disk **8:** 18, *19,* **9:** *29,* 30, 37
hardness **1:** 43–44, 45
harmonics **5:** 14, *15, 17,* 18
HDTV **7:** 45
hearing problems **5:** 39
hearing threshold **5:** *33*
heartbeat **9:** *12*
heat
  chemical energy **3:** 8
  clothing for **3:** *40*
  color change **3:** 35–36
  conduction 1: 15, **3:** 26–29, *37,* 40, (48–49), (51)
  convection 3: 30–33
  from electricity **3:** 8
  as energy 2: 27, *28,* **3:** 6–7
  friction **1:** 38
  latent 3: 18–19
  liquids **1:** 23
  magnetism **8:** 16
  mechanical energy **3:** 8–9
  production 3: 8–9
  radiation 3: 34–37
  solids **1:** 26–27
  sources **3:** *9*
  storage **3:** 17
  temperature 3: 10–11, *17*
  thermal conduction rate **3:** 28–29
  thermal conductivity **3:** *28,* 29, (48–49)
  trapping **3:** 40, *41*
  units **3:** 7
  vibration **3:** 6, 7
  see also temperature
heat capacity **3:** 16
heat capacity, specific 3: 16–17
heat exchanger **3:** *32,* 33
heat flow direction **3:** 10, 42
heat flow rate **3:** 28–29
heat pump **3:** 42–43
heat retention, vacuum bottle **3:** 39–40
heating, electric current **7:** 7, (49), **9:** 8–9
  power supply **7:** 23–24
  resistance **7:** 16, 18
  steelmaking **7:** 28
heating system, house **3:** 31, 33, 42–43
heavy water **10:** *8, 9,* 31, 32, (49–50)
heavy water reactor **10:** 32
hecto- (prefix) **2:** *9*
height **2:** 6
helical gears **2:** 45
heliosphere **8:** 15
helium **1:** *8,* 10, 18, 29, **10:** 15, 43, (46)
Henry, Joseph **8:** 25, 27, 28
Hero of Alexandria **3:** *23*
Hertz, Heinrich **7:** 36
hertz (Hz) **2:** *7,* **5:** 26
high jump **2:** *9*
high temperature measurement **3:** *15*
high-definition TV **7:** 45
high-voltage power-lines **7:** *6*
Hiroshima **10:** 29
hockey **2:** *18*
"hole" **9:** 18, *19,* 21–22
home computer **9:** 36–37
home electricity 7: 30–31
  energy consumption **7:** *17*
  meter **7:** 16–17
Hooke's law **1:** *44,* 45
horn, phonograph **5:** *37,* 42, (51)
hot (live) wire **7:** 31
hotness, and temperature 3: 10–11
hourglass **2:** *8*
house heating **3:** 31, 33
  heat pump **3:** 42–43
  insulation **3:** 29
Hubble Space Telescope **4:** *16,* **9:** 35
human body, isotopes **10:** 22–23
humpback whale **5:** *25*
hydraulic press **1:** 36–37
hydrogen **1:** 6, 10, 29, **6:** 39
  atom **6:** 34
  ions **6:** 34, 39
  isotopes **10:** 9, 12–13, 44, (48)
  liquid **10:** 18
  MRI imaging **8:** 19, *20*
  nucleus **10:** 9, 43, (46)
  scaled atom **9:** (46–47)
  water **10:** *9*
hydroxyl ions **6:** 39
ice **6:** *25*
  change of state **3:** 18, *19*
  density **1:** 18–19, 30
  expansion **1:** 30, **3:** 21, (48)
  freezing **1:** 30
  lifting **1:** (49)
  melting point **1:** 26, *30*
  thermal conductivity **3:** *28*
ice cores **10:** 23
ice hockey **2:** *18*
ice skater, friction **2:** *40*
icebergs **1:** 19
ice-breaker, nuclear **10:** *38*
idler gear **2:** 45
image
  colored fringes **4:** *32*
  curved mirror **4:** 16–17
  fuzzy **4:** 33
  plane mirror **4:** 14–15
  rainbow **4:** 29
  real **4:** 15
  reversal **4:** 29, (50)
  virtual **4:** 15
imaging **8:** 19–20
impurity semiconductors **9:** 17–19, 25
incandescent bulb *see* electric light
incident ray **4:** 14, 18
inclines 2: *11,* 40–41
indium **9:** 27
induction, transformer **7:** 20–21
induction charge **6:** *12,* 13, 20
induction furnace **7:** 28
induction motor **8:** 36–37, *40*
Industrial Revolution **1:** 33
industrial x-rays **10:** 22
industrialization, electric power **8:** 39
inert gas, lighting **4:** 7, **7:** 19
inertia **2:** 20
  checkers **2:** (48)
  moving objects **2:** (48–49)
infrared photograph **3:** 37, *38*
infrared radiation **3:** 35, *37*
  wavelength change **3:** 40, *41*
infrasound *see* subsonic vibration
input devices, computers **9:** 37
instruments, optical 4: 36–41
insulator
  atomic structure **3:** 27, 28
  ceramic **6:** 19
  electric **7:** 9, (46)
  high-voltage **6:** 19
  static charge **6:** 6–7
  testing **6:** 14
  thermal conductivity **3:** *28,* 29
integrated circuit
  embedded **9:** 33, 34–35
  interconnects **9:** 27
  manufacture 9: 24–27
  quality testing **9:** 27
  size limit **9:** 45
interconnects, circuit **9:** 27
interference, light **4:** 42–44
interlacing, TV picture **7:** *44*
intermolecular forces **1:** 14, 15
internal combustion engine **1:** 34–35
Internet **5:** 45, **9:** 42
Inuit **3:** *29*
inverse square law **6:** 10, **8:** 11
iodine, sublimation **3:** 18
ionic bond **1:** *7,* 15, **6:** 34, 36
ionization, air **6:** 23, *24,* **10:** *23*
ionosphere **6:** 35, **7:** *37*
ions 1: 7, 15, **6:** 34–35, **7:** 6
  atoms **6:** 34–35
  attraction **6:** 34
  charge **6:** 34, 35
  crystals **6:** 11, *35*
  dissolved 6: 36–37, (50–51)
  electric charge **6:** 38, (50)
  electron transfer **6:** *35*
  formation **6:** *35*
  moving 6: 38–39, **10:** 10
  potato power **6:** (49–50)
  producing electricity **6:** 42
  recombination **6:** 35
  semiconductors **9:** 18
iris **4:** 34
iron
  alloys **1:** 45
  magnetic **8:** 7, 11
iron filings **8:** *8,* 10, (46–47), (50)
iron-nickel core **5:** 31
isotopes 10: 10–11
  and atoms **10:** 9–11, (47–48)
  decay **10:** (47–48)
  nonradioactive **10:** 23
  odd and even rule **10:** 11
  separating **10:** 12–13
  uses **10:** 22–23
  whole number rule **10:** 11

J

jackhammers **1:** 32, *35*
jackscrew **2:** *41*
jazz percussionist **5:** *20*
jet airliners **1:** 40
jet engines **1:** 32–33, 35
Joliot-Curie, Irène **10:** 24
Joliot-Curie, Jean-Frédéric **10:** 24
joule **2:** *7,* 30–31, **3:** 7, 16
Joule, James **3:** 17
Joule-Kelvin effect **3:** 42, 45
Joule's law **3:** 17
Joule-Thomson effect **3:** 42, 45
junction diode **9:** *21*
junction transistor **9:** *21, 22*

K

kapok **3:** *28*
Kelvin, Lord (William Thomson) **3:** 11
Kelvin scale **2:** *7,* **3:** 11, 15
kettledrum **5:** 21, *22,* 23
kilo- (prefix) **2:** 7, *9*
kilobyte (kB) **9:** 28
kilocalorie (kcal) **3:** 7, 16
kilogram (kg) **2:** *7,* 11
kilowatt (kW) **7:** 16
kilowatt-hour **7:** 16
kinetic energy **2:** 27, *28, 29*
  potential energy conversion **2:** *29,* 30
kite **6:** *23*
klystron **9:** *11,* 13
Kornei, Otto **6:** 28
krypton **10:** 28

L

lakes, freezing **3:** 21–22
land breeze **3:** 31
Landsat satellite **3:** 37
land-speed record **5:** *24*
larynx **5:** 40, *41*
laser 4: *12,* 42–45
  CD **5:** *44*
  CD-ROM **9:** 31
  coherent **4:** 44, *45*
  light rays 4: 42–45
laser fusion **10:** 45, *45*
laser microscope **9:** *41*
latent heat 3: 18–19
  condensation **3:** 18
  freezing **3:** 18
  fusion **3:** 18
  vaporization **3:** 18, *19,* 42
lateral inversion **4:** 15
lava **1:** *26*
Lawrence, E. O. **10:** 24
laws of motion *see* Newton's laws of motion
LCD (liquid-crystal display) **9:** 39
lead **3:** 25
leaks, radioactivity **10:** *23*
Leaning Tower of Pisa **2:** *14*
Leclanché, Georges **6:** 44
Leclanché cell **6:** 44
LED (light-emitting diode) **7:** 45, **9:** *20,* 33
left-hand motor rule **8:** 32
length
  pitch **5:** 13, (50)
  resistance **7:** 15, (51)
lens 4: 13
  action 4: 30–33
  concave **4:** 31
  convex **4:** 30, *31*
  faulty **4:** *32,* 33
  human eye **4:** 34
  longsight **4:** 35
  shortsight **4:** 35
  water as **4:** (50), (50–51)
LEP (Large Electron-Positron Collider) **10:** 26–27
levers 2: 36–39
  class 1 **2:** 36, *37,* 38–39
  class 2 **2:** 36, *37, 38*
  class 3 **2:** 36–37
  loads 2: 36–39
  mechanical advantage **2:** 38, 39
  mechanical efficiency **2:** 39
  springy **2:** *36*
Leyden jar **6:** 17
LHC (Large Hadron Collector) **10:** 26–27
Liebig, Justus von **1:** *31*
Liebig condenser **1:** *31*
lift **1:** 40–41, *41,* (49), (50)
light 4: 18–21, 24–29
  color 4: 24–29, **6:** 32
  color mixing **4:** 25–27
  conversion to electricity **4:** 8–9
  as energy 2: 27, *28,* 29, **4:** 8–9
  gravity **2:** *12*
  interference **4:** 42–44
  monochromatic **4:** 42–44
  particle **4:** 11
  production 4: 6–7
  propagation 4: 10–11
  reflection 4: 14–17, (48)
  refraction 4: 18–21, (48–49)
  scattering **4:** (47)
  speed 4: 12–13
  ultraviolet **6:** 32, *33*
  wavelength **4:** 42
light rays 4: 42–45
light waves 4: 11
  coherent **4:** 44–45
  lasers 4: 42–45
light-emitting diode (LED) **7:** 45, **9:** *20,* 33
lightning 6: 22–25
  artificial **6:** 19
  charge separation **6:** *24*
  clouds **6:** 22, 23, *24, 25*
  danger **6:** 23, 25

frequency 6: 22
heating effect 6: 24
high-voltage spark 6: 35
protection 6: 24–25
thunder delay 5: 25
lightning conductor 6: 15, 24–25
linacs 10: 25–26
Linde process 3: 45
linear expansion (expansivity) 3: 25
linear induction motor 8: 37, 40
linemen 7: *6, 34*
lips 5: 19, 41
liquefied petroleum gas 1: 10
liquid 1: 12–13, 26–27, 36–37
apparent expansion 3: 21
boiling point 1: 23
conductors 6: 37
convection 3: 31, 33, (49)
cooling 1: 30, (49)
density 1: 12
depth 1: 12
electrostatic charge 6: 27
elements 1: 6
expansion 3: 20–22, (47)
heating 1: 23
molecules 1: 12–13, 23, 30, 36
pressure 1: 12, 36–37
purity 1: 24
surface tension 1: 13
viscosity 1: 13
see also fluids
liquid-crystal display (LCD) 9: 39
liquid-in-glass thermometer 3: *12,* 13
liquid microscope 4: (50–51)
liquid sodium 10: 33
lithium 10: 24, 45, (46)
live wire 7: 31
loads 2: 36–39
locomotive *see* train
lodestone 8: 6–7, 16
long waves 7: *37,* 38
longsight 4: 35
Los Alamos 10: 31
loudhailer 5: *37*
loudness of sound 5: 32–33
loudspeaker 5: 27, *45,* 8: 30, *31*
low-temperature thermometers 3: 13
lubricants 2: 41, 3: 9

M

Mach number 5: 25
magenta 4: 26
maglev train 3: 45, 8: *42, 43,* 45
magma 1: *26*
magnesium 6: 41
salts 6: 37
magnet
ammeter 7: *13*
forces between 8: *9, 10*
loudspeaker 5: *45*
making 8: 7, 16–17
strength 8: 11, (46)
superconduction 8: *43,* 45
uses 8: 18–21
see also electromagnet
magnetic bearings 8: 43
magnetic domains 8: 7, 16, *17,* 9: 30
magnetic field 8: 8–11, *9,* (46–47)
alpha radiation 10: 15
alternating 7: 20
beta radiation 10: 15
blocking 8: (47)
charged particles 10: 10
closed loop 8: 10
cyclotron 10: 24
direction 8: 10, *25*
Earth 8: 12–15, (49)
electric current 7: 7, 8: *22, 23*
field line shape 8: *11*
gamma radiation 10: 15
mapping 8: 9–10
motor effect 8: 32–33
picturing 8: 8, 10, *13*
plasma 10: *44*
plotting 8: 9–10
reversal 8: 15
saturation 8: 7, 24
shielding 8: (47)
strength 8: 11, 24
Sun 8: 15
tape recording 5: *43,* 44
magnetic field coil 8: 41
magnetic field lines, Earth 8: *13*
magnetic imaging 8: 19–20
magnetic lift 8: (48)
magnetic materials 8: 6–7, 11
magnetic mine 8: 25–26
magnetic north 8: 12, *13*
magnetic poles 8: 8–11
Earth's 8: 12–15, (49)
magnetic recording 5: 43–44, 8: 19
magnetic resonance imaging (MRI) 8: 19–20
magnetic sensors, car 8: 30
magnetic storage 9: 29–30
magnetism
animal navigation 8: 14, *15*
attraction 8: 9, *10, 11,* (48), (48–49)
Earth's 8: 12–15, (49)
electricity 7: 7, 8: 22–23
loss 8: 16
in solenoids 8: 23
magnetosphere 8: 14–15
magnetron 9: 13
magnification 4: 17, 30, *31, 32,* 33
Maksutov telescope 4: *39*
malleability 1: 15
manometer 1: *10*
mantle
Earth 5: 31
gas light 4: *7*
mapping
magnetic field 8: 9–10
undersea 5: *35*
Marconi, Guglielmo 7: 36–37
marine life 3: 21–22
masking, integrated circuits 9: 26, 27
mass 1: 18, 2: 11–13
comparison 2: 12
conversion to weight 2: 12
pendulum 2: 24–25
units 2: 11
and weight 2: 11–12
mass spectrograph 10: 10, 11, 12–13
mass spectrometer 10: 11
mass spectroscope 10: 11
mass storage 9: 29–31
massively parallel computing 9: *33,* 34
materials
magnetic 8: 6–7
sound conduction 5: 11, 25, (46–47)
matter
measurement 2: 6–9
states of 1: 8
maximum and minimum thermometer 3: *15*
Maxwell, James Clerk 7: 36
measurement 2: 6–9
mechanical advantage 2: 37–38, *39*
bottle opener 2: *39*
calculation 2: 39
class 1 lever 2: 38
crowbar 2: 38
pulley 2: 43
shears 2: *39*
wedge 2: 40
windlass 2: *38,* 39
mechanical efficiency 2: 39
mechanical energy, heat from 3: 8–9
medical images 3: 35, 5: *27,* 8: 19–20
medium waves 7: *37,* 38
mega- (prefix) 2: *9*
megabyte (MB) 9: 28
Meitner, Lise 10: 28
meltdown 10: 33
melting 1: 26, 27, 3: 18, *19,* 6: 37
melting point 1: 14, 26–27, *30*
membrane, drums 5: 21
memory, electronic 9: 28–31
meniscus 1: 13
mercury 1: 6
barometer 1: 8, 9–10
boiling point 1: 23
expansion 3: *21*
fluorescent tubes 6: 32
freezing point 3: *11*
latent heat of vaporization 3: *19*
manometer 1: *10*
melting point 1: 26
meniscus 1: 13
motor effect 8: 32–33
thermometer 3: *12,* 13
volume expansivity 3: 21
mercury oxide cell 6: 44
mercury vapor 4: *6, 7*
mesh dishes 7: *36*
metal
alloys 1: 45
bimetallic strip 3: 13–14
boiling point 1: 23
bonding 1: 15
breaking point 1: *44*
cooling 1: 31
crystalline 1: 6, 7, 15
ductility 1: 15, 45
elasticity 1: 44–45
electrolysis 6: 41
elements 1: 6
extraction 6: 41, (51)
hardness 1: 45
heat conduction 3: 26–27, (48–49), (51)
ions 6: 34
liquid 10: *33*
magnetic 8: 11, (48–49)
malleability 1: 15
purification 6: (51)
separation 8: 21
strength 1: 19, 43–44
see also electrical conduction
metal detectors 8: *23*
meteorite 2: 30
meter (unit) 2: 7, *7*
methane 1: *7,* 10
metric prefixes 2: 7, *9*
metric system 2: 7, 9
Michelson method, speed of light 4: 12–13
micro- (prefix) 2: *9*
microchip
manufacture 9: 24–27
optical 9: 45
size 9: *24*
size limit 9: 45
smart card 9: *28*
uses 9: 32–35
micrometer 2: *8*
microphone 5: *44,* 7: 34, 8: 31
microscope 4: 39–40, (50–51), 9: *41*
microscopic plants 4: *41*
microwave oven 9: *45*
microwave production 9: 13
microwave radio 7: *36*
microwaves 3: *37*
miles, unit differences 2: 6–7
Milky Way 10: *42*
milli- (prefix) 2: *9*
millibar 1: 36
Millikan, Robert 9: 8
mine, magnetic 8: 25–26
mine tunnel 7: 10
minerals 1: 15
miners' safety lamp 3: *28*
mirage 4: 20–21
mirror 1: 15
curved 4: *14,* 15–17
image formation 4: 14–17
laser 4: 45
light scattering 4: (47)
multiple reflection 4: (46)
plane 4: 14–15, *16*
as prism 4: (46–47)
rainbow 4: (46–47)
solar energy 7: 26–27
space telescope 4: *16*
mirror telescopes 4: 38–39
mobile 2: *32*
mobile phone 7: 39–40, 9: 42
cells 7: 40–41
models for testing 1: 41
moderator 10: 31, 32, *34*
modulation, signals 7: 38–39, 44
mole (mol) 2: *7*
molecular weight 1: 24
molecules 1: 6–7
air 6: 23, *24*
cooling 1: 28
crystals 1: 15
gases 1: 13, 36
liquids 1: 12, 23, 30, 36
melting 1: *27*
shapes 1: *7*
solids 1: 14, 26
water 6: 37
molecules, motion
electrical conduction 3: 27
expansion 3: 24–25
heat conduction 3: 27, 28
sound waves 5: 7–8, *9*
moment *see* torque; turning moment
momentum 2: 20–21
monkey wrench 2: 34, *35*
monochromatic light 4: 42–43, 44
monorail 8: *42, 43*
Moon
distance measurement 4: *12*
eclipse 4: 10, *11*
gravity 2: 11
orbit 2: 22–23
orbital force 2: 22–23
Moon-Earth forces 2: 19
Morse, Samuel 7: 32, 8: 29
Morse code 7: 32, *33,* 8: 29
mothballs 1: 27
motion
circular 2: 22–23
force 2: 18
inertia 2: 20
Netwon's laws 2: 18–20
motor, electric *see* electric motor
motor effect 8: 32–33
motor rule 8: 32
motorbike 9: *34*
mouse 9: 36, 37
mouth, shaping sounds 5: 41
mouthpiece
antinode 5: 18
telephone 7: 34, *35*
movies 4: 41, 9: 41
moving-coil meters 7: 12, 13
MP3 5: 45
MRI (magnetic resonance imaging) 8: 19–20
multiple reflections 4: (46)
multiple snowflakes 4: *30*
music
electronic 9: 45
and noise 5: *6–7*
note ratios 5: 13
portable 5: *42*
musical instruments

  - percussion **5:** 20–23
  - prehistoric **5:** 20
  - string **5:** 12–15
  - vibrating air **5:** 16–19

N

- Nagasaki **10:** 29
- nano- (prefix) **2:** *9*
- naphthalene **1:** 27
- natural gas **1:** 29
- navigation
  - aircraft **9:** *43,* 44–45
  - animal **8:** 14, *15*
  - bats **5:** *27*
- neon **1:** 29, **6:** 32, **10:** 10, (46)
- networked computers **9:** *38*
- neutral equilibrium **2:** 32–33
- neutral wire **7:** 31
- neutralization, charge **6:** 15
- neutrinos **10:** *43*
- neutron **10:** *7*
  - decay **10:** 18
  - emission **10:** 17–18
  - nucleus **10:** 9, 11, (46)
  - protons **10:** 18
  - radiation **10:** 17–18
  - radioisotopes **10:** 39
- news photographers **4:** *37*
- Newton, Sir Isaac **2:** 19
  - light spectrum **4:** 22, *23*
  - orbiting bodies **2:** 22–23
- newton (unit) **2:** *7,* 11
- Newtonian telescope **4:** *39*
- newtonmeters **2:** 13
- Newton's laws of motion **2:** 18–21
  - conservation of momentum **2:** 20–21
  - first **2:** 18–19
  - second **2:** 19
  - third **2:** 19–20
- Newton's rings **4:** 43–44
- nickel, magnetic **8:** 11
- nickel-cadmium cell **6:** 44
- NIFE cell **6:** *45*
- nitrogen **1:** 8, 29
  - isotope **10:** *21,* 24
  - liquid **3:** *11*
  - nucleus **10:** (46)
- *n*-material production **9:** 27
- node
  - flute **5:** *19*
  - pipe **5:** *17,* 18–19
  - string **5:** *13*
  - woodwinds **5:** *18*
- noise, and music **5:** *6–7*
- noise pollution **5:** 33
- non metals, magnetism **8:** (48–49)
- normal **4:** 14, *18*
- north, magnetic **8:** 12, *13*
- north-seeking pole **8:** 9, 23
- *n-p-n* transistor **9:** 22
- *n*-type semiconductor **9:** 18, *21,* (50)
- nuclear bombs **10:** *12,* 13, 19
- **nuclear energy** **2:** *28,* 29, **3:** *9,* **7:** 23, **10:** 36–39
  - chain reaction **10:** *30*
  - dangers **7:** 26, **10:** 33–35, 38
  - environment **10:** 37
  - Sun **10:** 42–43
  - **waste** **10:** 40–41
- **nuclear fission** **10:** 28–29, 42, (51)
  - energy **10:** 31
  - peaceful use **10:** 30
  - ships **10:** 38
  - **waste** **10:** 40–41
- **nuclear fusion** **10:** 42, (51)
  - **controlled** **10:** 44–45
  - deuterium **10:** *43,* (51)
  - protons **10:** 43
  - Sun **10:** *43*
  - tritium **10:** *43,* (51)
- nuclear fusion reactors **10:** 44
  - plasma **10:** *45*
  - stars as **10:** *42, 43*
- nuclear ice-breaker **10:** *38*
- nuclear power stations **10:** 19, *36, 37*
- **nuclear reactors** **10:** 17, 30–35
  - biological shield **10:** 36, 38–39
  - containment buildings **10:** *34, 36,* 37
  - coolants **10:** 31, *32, 33, 34,* 36
  - fuel reprocessing **10:** 41
  - fuel rods **10:** 36–37, 40–41
  - graphite **10:** 30–31
  - models **10:** (50–51)
  - moderator **10:** 31, 32
  - types **10:** 31–33, 36, *39,* 40
- nuclear transformation **10:** *21*
- nucleons **10:** *7*
- nucleus **1:** 6
  - atoms **6:** 6, 11
  - charge **6:** 11, **10:** *7*
  - discovery **9:** 7
  - neutrons **10:** 9, (46)
  - protons **10:** 9, 11, (46)
  - radiation **10:** 14–19
  - radioactivity **10:** 11
  - stability **10:** 11

O

- Oak Ridge, Tennessee **10:** *12*
- objective lens **4:** 38, 39–40
- **objects, falling** **2:** 14–15
- oboe **5:** 19
- ocean **1:** *25,* **6:** *36,* 37–38
  - black smokers **3:** (49)
  - convection **3:** 33
  - cores from bed **10:** 23
- Oersted, Hans Christian **8:** 22, 23
- ohm **2:** *7,* **7:** 10
- Ohm, Georg **7:** 15
- Ohm's law **7:** 14–15
- oil **2:** 41, **6:** 37, **10:** 37, 38
- oil film colors **4:** 43, (49)
- oil lamp **4:** 6–7
- oil pipeline, expansion **3:** 24
- oil refinery **1:** 10
- oil tanker fire **6:** *8*
- opera glasses **4:** 38
- optical chips **9:** 45
- optical fibers **4:** 21
- **optical instruments** **4:** 36–41
- orange oil **4:** 49
- orbitals **9:** *7,* 14, 17
- orchestra **5:** *12*
- organ *see* pipe organ
- oscilloscope **9:** 11, *12*
- otitis **5:** 39
- output devices **9:** 37–38
- oven, microwave **9:** *45*
- overhead power lines, expansion **3:** 24
- oxidation oven **9:** 26
- oxide ion **6:** 34
- oxyacetylene welding **1:** 10
- oxygen **1:** 6, 8, 29, 35, **6:** 34, 39
  - atomic number **10:** 11
  - boiling **3:** *11*
  - freezing **3:** *11*
  - nucleus **10:** (46)
  - plant production **4:** 8
  - water **10:** *9*

P

- P (push-pull) waves **5:** 31
- pain threshold, noise **5:** *33*
- paint, mixing colors **4:** 27–28
- paint sprays **6:** 27, *28*
- palmtop computers **9:** *37,* 39
- Pan pipes **5:** (47)
- Pangaea **8:** 15
- pantograph **7:** *8,* **8:** 45
- paper amplifier **5:** (51)
- paper cup, clucking sound **5:** (48)
- parachute **2:** 15, *21*
- parallel circuit **7:** 11, 15, *16,* (50)
- parallel computing **9:** *33,* 34
- parallelogram of vectors **2:** *17*
- parka **3:** *29*
- partial eclipse **4:** *11*
- particle accelerator **6:** *21,* **10:** 24, 25
- particle detectors **8:** 21
- particle nature of light **4:** 11
- **particles** **1:** 6, 15
  - electric charge **6:** 31, **10:** 10, 42–43
  - **movement** **1:** 8–11
  - nucleons **10:** *7*
  - subatomic **10:** 17, 18
  - Sun **10:** 42–43
  - tracks **10:** *18*
- pascal **1:** 36
- **PC (personal computer)** **8:** 18–19, **9:** 36–39
- PCB (printed circuit board) **9:** 24–25, *27*
- Peierls, Rudolf **10:** 29
- pendulum clock **2:** 25
- **pendulum swing** **2:** 24–25, (51)
  - energy **2:** 30
  - Galileo's experiments **2:** 24–25
- penny whistle **5:** 17, *18*
- pentaprism **4:** *23, 37*
- percussion **5:** *20, 22*
- periscope **4:** 15, *16*
- **personal computer (PC)** **8:** 18–19, **9:** 36–39
- peta- (prefix) **2:** *9*
- phone *see* telephone
- phonograph **5:** *37,* 42
- phosphor **6:** 32, *33,* **7:** *43,* 44
- phosphorus **6:** 27, **9:** 27
- photoconductor **6:** 28
- photocopying **6:** 28–29, **9:** 40
- photoelectric cell **4:** 8–9
- photoelectricity **7:** 27, 28–29
- photons **10:** *43*
- photoresist **9:** *25,* 26, 27
- photosynthesis **4:** 8
- pico- (prefix) **2:** *9*
- pigments, mixing **4:** 27–28
- pin-hole camera **4:** (51)
- pinion **2:** 45
- pinna **5:** 38, *39*
- pints, unit differences **2:** *7*
- pipe organ **5:** *16,* 17
- pipeline **1:** 39, **3:** 24
- pipes **5:** *17,* 18, 19
- pipes of Pan **5:** (47)
- Pisa, Leaning Tower **2:** *14*
- piston **1:** 33, 34, 36–37
- pitch **5:** *11*
  - larynx **5:** 40
  - penny whistle **5:** 17, *18*
  - pipes **5:** 19
  - string orchestra **5:** *12*
- pitchblende **10:** 16, 40
- pithead winding gear **8:** *38*
- pivot **2:** 33–34, (47)
  - *see also* fulcrum
- plane mirror **4:** 14–15
- plano-convex lens **4:** *44*
- plasma **10:** 43, 44, *45*
- plastics **1:** 14, 44, **6:** 27
  - chlorine gas **6:** *38*
  - drinks bottle **1:** (46–47)
  - electrical insulators **7:** 9
  - sprayed on **6:** 27
  - thermal conductivity **3:** 29
- platinum resistance thermometer **3:** *12,* 15
- plosives **5:** *41*
- plotting magnetic field **8:** 9–10
- plutonium **10:** 13, 29, 32, *33*
- *p-n-p* transistor **9:** 22
- point charge fields **6:** 15, *16*
- polar lights **8:** *12*
- polar solvent, water **6:** 37
- polarization, battery **6:** 43–44
- pole vaulting **2:** *36*
- poles, geographical **8:** 12, *13*
- poles, magnetic *see* magnetic poles
- pollution
  - atmospheric **6:** *26*
  - energy generation **7:** 26
  - fuels **6:** 26–27
  - greenhouse gases **10:** 37–38
  - power stations **10:** 37
- polonium **10:** 16, *21*
- polymers **1:** 14
- pond skaters **1:** 13
- portable computer **9:** *37,* 39
- positron **9:** 15, **10:** 17, *26, 43*
- positron emission tomography **10:** 17
- potassium salts **6:** 37
- **potential difference** **7:** 8–11, 14–15
  - *see also* voltage
- potential energy **2:** *26,* 27, *28, 29,* 30
- **power** **2:** 27–31
  - and efficiency **2:** 39
  - **electrical** **7:** 14–17, 18–19
- power (energy) consumption **7:** *17*
- power lines, expansion **3:** 24
- power station **1:** *28,* 35, **10:** 37
- power steering **8:** 30
- power switch **7:** *30*
- power transmission, mechanical **2:** 43–45
- precipitator, electrostatic **6:** 26–27
- prefixes, metric **2:** 7, *9*
- pregnancy, scan **5:** *27*
- **pressure** **1:** 32–35, 36–37
  - air **1:** 32–35, (46–47), (50)
  - atmospheric **1:** 8, 9
  - boiling point **1:** 23–24
  - fluids **1:** 39
  - gas **1:** 8, 10–11, 28, 32–35, **3:** 23
  - gas liquefaction **3:** 43
  - liquid **1:** 12, 36–37
  - measuring ***1:*** *9, 10,* 36
  - melting point **1:** 27
  - sublimation **3:** 18
  - Sun's center **10:** 42–43
- pressure coefficient **3:** 22–23
- Pressurized-Water Reactor **10:** 31–32, *33, 39*
- primary colors
  - light **4:** 26
  - pigments **4:** 27
  - TV camera **7:** 43–44
- printed circuit board (PCB) **9:** 24–25, *27*
- printer **6:** 27, **9:** 37–38
- printing, subtractive **4:** 27–28
- **prisms** **4:** 13, 22–23
  - **action** **4:** 22–23
  - binoculars **4:** 38
  - water as **4:** (46–47)
- projector **4:** 40–41
- **propagation of light** **4:** 10–11
- propellants **1:** 35, **3:** 23
- propeller, ship **1:** 29
- proton
  - acceleration **10:** 24
  - Big Bang **10:** 7

  fusion 10: 43
  neutrons 10: 18
  nucleus 10: 9, 11, (46)
  repulsion 10: 11
  scale 9: (46–47)
p-type semiconductor 9: 19, *21*, 27
  modeling 9: (51)
publishing 9: 38
pulleys 2: 42–45
  gears 2: 42–45
  mechanical advantage 2: 43
  pithead gear 8: *38*
pump 1: 20, 36, 37
pure sound 5: *39*
purification, metals 6: 41, (51)
purity/boiling point 1: 24
purse, radiograph 10: *19*
push-pull (compression) waves 5: 8, *9*
pyramids 2: 40
pyrometer 3: *15*
Pythagoras 5: 13

Q

quantum computer 9: 45
quantum theory 9: 9, 10: *7*
quartz 3: 25
quartz-halogen lamps 7: 19

R

racing cars, smart 9: 35
rack and pinion 2: 45
radar *9: 11*, 13
radar sets 6: 41
radiation 6: 35, 10: 14–19
  background 10: 19
  and color 3: 39–40
  electromagnetic 10: 14, 15, *16, 17*
  heat 3: 34–37
  neutrons 10: 17–18
  nucleus 10: 14–19
  reflected 3: 40
  from Sun 4: 8, 9
  ultraviolet 6: 35
  vacuum bottle 3: 40
  x-rays 6: 33
radiation sickness 10: 15
radiation therapy 10: 16, 23
radiator
  car 3: *32*
  house 3: *33*
radio communications 7: 36–37, 38–41
  digital signals 7: 41
  distortion 7: 39
  mobile phone 7: 39–40
  modulation 7: 38–39
  signal reflection 7: *37*
radio signals 9: (47)
radio wave 3: *37*, 6: 35, 7: *37*
radioactive decay 10: 16, 20–21, (48–49)
  alpha particles 10: 16, *21*
  half-life 10: 20, (48–49)
  radiation therapy 10: 23
  radon 10: 20
  uranium 10: 20
radioactive waste 10: 37, 40–41
radioactivity 10: 14–19
  airborne 10: *34*
  gas leaks 10: *23*
  Geiger counter *10: 14, 15*
  natural 10: 15, 19
  nuclear bombs 10: 19
  nucleus 10: 11
  purse 10: *19*
  threat 10: *28*
  see also nuclear energy; nuclear reactors
radiocarbon-dating 10: 20–21
radioisotopes 10: 17, *22*, 23, 39
radiotelephony 7: 38–41
radium 10: 16
radius of curvature 4: 16
radon 10: 19, 20
railroad tracks, expansion 3: 24, *25*
rain 6: *25*
rainbow 4: *28*, (46–47)
rainbow colors 4: *22*
raindrop, dispersion 4: 29
rainwater 1: 25
RAM (random-access memory) 9: 28–29, 37
rapid-transit systems 8: 44
rarefied waves 5: 8, *9*
reaction motors 1: 35
read-only memory 9: 29, 37
real focus 4: 16
real image 4: 15, 16–17
receiver, radiotelephony 7: *39*
recombination, ions 6: 35
record player 5: *37*, 42
recorder 5: *18*
recording
  CD 5: 44–45
  electronic 5: 43
  magnetic 5: 43–44, 8: 19
  mechanical 5: 42
  sound 5: 42–45
recording studio 5: *45*
record/replay head 5: 43–44
records 5: 42
rectifier 9: 10, *13, 22, 33*
  half-wave 9: (49)
recycling trash 6: 13
reducing glass 4: 33
reeds 5: 17, (48–49)
reflecting telescope 4: 38–39
reflection of light
  laws 4: 14, *15*
  multiple 4: (46)
reflection of sound 5: 34–35
refraction of light 4: 18–21
  apparent depth 4: (48–49)
  refracted ray 4: 18
refraction of sound 5: 36–37
refractive index 4: 18
refrigeration 1: 29, 3: 42, *44*
regenerative braking 8: 43, *45*
registration, cellphone 7: 39–40, 9: 42
relative atomic mass 10: *10*, 11
relativity 10: 27
relay 8: 29–30, *31*
renewable energy 7: 26–27, 10: 38, 44
reproduction, sound 5: 42–45
  paper amplifier 5: (51)
repulsion 6: 8–11, (48–49)
  electric currents 8: *22*, 23
  magnetic 8: *9, 10, 11*
  protons 10: 11
resistance, electrical 7: 10–11, 14–17
  area/length 7: 15, (51)
  changing 7: 18–19
  crystal structure 7: 18
  heating 7: *7*, 16, 18, 23–24
  Ohm's law 7: 14–15
  power 7: 14–17
  series/parallel 7: 11, 15, *16*
  and temperature 7: 15
  variable 7: *18*, 19
  see also superconductivity
resonance 5: 29–30
resonator, xylophone 5: 21
resultant 2: *17*
retina 4: *34*, 35
reversing arrow 4: (50)
rheostat 7: *18*, 19
Richter scale 5: 30
rifle, action and reaction 2: *19*
ring circuit 7: *31*
rivers 1: *25*
road bridge, expansion 3: *24*, 25
robot arms 9: *32*, 33
rock 1: 15, 44
  continental drift 8: 15
  cores 10: 23
  examination 4: 40
  radiocarbon-dating 10: 20–21
rock salt 1: 16
rocket, reaction motor 1: 35, 2: 19–20
rocket balloon 2: (49)
Roentgen, Wilhelm 6: 33, 9: 14
roller coaster 2: *29*
rollers, friction 2: (50)
ROM (read-only memory) 9: 29, 37
Roosevelt, Franklin D. 10: 28–29
rope drive 2: 43
rotary generator 6: 19–20
rotation 2: 22–23
  electric motor 8: 33
  see also torque; turning moment
rotor 7: 23, 8: 36
routing, telephone system 7: 35
rubber 1: 44
rubber band, sound conduction 5: (46–47)
ruby 1: 16, 4: *45*
ruler, sounds from 5: (50)
Rumford, Count (Benjamin Thompson) 3: 8–9, 9
Rutherford, Ernest 9: 7, 10: *6–7*

S

S (shear) waves 5: 31
safety lamp 3: *28*
St. Paul's Cathedral 5: *10*
salt, common *see* sodium chloride
salts 1: 15, 6: 35, 37
sampling, CD 5: 45
satellite
  GPS 9: 43–44
  infrared pictures 3: 37
  orbit 2: 23
  radiation detection 9: 15
satellite communications 7: *37*, 40–41
  phone 9: 42
  time delay 7: 41
  UHF band 7: 39
saturation, magnetic 8: 7, 24
Saturn 2: *23*
Saturn V rocket 1: 35, 5: *32*
saxophone 5: 19
scalars 2: 16–17, 21
scan, MRI 8: 19–20
scanner 9: 37, *44*
scanning, TV 7: *44*
scattering of light 4: (47)
Schmidt camera 4: *39*
scissors 2: 36
scrap separation 8: 21
screaming sound, cellophane 5: (48–49)
screw 2: 39, 41
screwdriver, couples 2: 35
sea *see* ocean
sea breeze 3: 31
sea turtle, x-ray 9: *15*
seawater plants 4: *41*
second (s) 2: *7*
secondary colors 4: 26, 27
secondary rainbow 4: *28*, 29
seesaw 2: 33–34, (47)
seismic waves 5: 30–31
semicircular canals 5: 39
semiconductors
  chip manufacture 9: 24–27
  impurities 9: 17–19
  materials 9: 16–19
  modeling 9: (51)
  solar cell 7: *29*
  solid-state devices 9: 20–23
sensors, car 8: 30
separation
  centrifugal 10: 13
  electromagnetic 10: 13
  gas-diffusion 10: 13
  isotopes 10: 12–13
  scrap 8: 21
series circuit 7: (50)
  current flow 7: 11
  resistors 7: 15, *16*
server 9: *38*
sextant 2: *8*
shadow, Earth 4: 10–11
shadow zone 5: *31*
shadowmask CRT 7: *43*, 44
shakedown 5: *28*
shape, and resistance 7: 15
shark 1: *38*
shear 1: *44*
shears 2: 36, *39*
sheet lightning 6: 22
shellac 5: 42
shells, electrons 9: 17
  see also orbitals
ship tank 1: 41
ships 1: 11, 21, 29, 39, 5: *36*, 10: 38
shock proof 6: *19*
Shockley, William 9: 18
shock-wave cone 5: *24*
shooting
  action and reaction 2: *19*
  ear protectors 5: *33*
shopper thermograph 3: *34*
short waves 7: *37*
shortsight 4: 31, 35
shutter 4: 36
SI system 2: *7*, 9
signal boosting, telegraph 8: 29–30
silicon 9: *16*, 17, 25–27
silicon dioxide coating 9: 26
silver, thermal conductivity 3: *28*
silver plating 6: 40
simple camera 4: *36*
simulated starlight 4: *45*
single-lens reflex camera 4: *23*, 37
siren, Doppler effect 5: *25*
size/weight 1: 18
skateboarder 5: *42*
skater, friction 2: *40*
skins, vibrating 5: 20–23, (48)
skydivers 2: *15*
slide projector 4: 40–41
slip rings 8: *35*
slope *see* inclines
smart bike 9: *34*
smart card 9: *28*
smart vehicles 9: 34–35
smoke detector 10: *23*
Snell, Willebrord 4: 21
Snell's law 4: 18–19
snow 1: 25, 30
snowflake 3: *43*, 4: *30*
soap bubbles 4: 43, (49)
society, impact of electronics 9: 40–45
socket wrench, couples 2: 35
sodium 1: 7, 6: *35*, 10: 9, 33
sodium chloride 1: 7, 15, 16, 24, *30*, 6: 34, 35
  crystals 6: *35*
  dissolved 6: 36, 37
  molten 6: *39*
  seas 6: 37–38
  seawater 6: 37–38
sodium cyanide 6: 40

soft magnetic metal **8:** 24, 36
solar cell **3:** 37, **7:** *29*
solar energy **3:** 37, **7:** 26–27, 28–29
solar furnace **3:** *36,* 37, **4:** *14*
solar heating **3:** *9*
solar panel **4:** 9, **9:** *42*
solar wind **8:** 14–15
solenoid **8:** 22, *23*
  bar magnets **8:** 23
  electric bell **8:** 28–29
  electromagnetism **8:** 23, 24
  magnetic field **7:** 12
solids **1:** 14–17, 26–27, 42–45
  amorphous **1:** 14, 30
  atoms **1:** 14, 26
  bonding **1:** 15
  cooling **1:** 15, 30
  crystalline **1:** 14, 15, 30, **6:** 36
  expansion **3:** 21, 24–25
  hardness **1:** 43–44
  heat **1:** 26–27
  melting points **1:** 14
  molecules **1:** 14, 26
  noncrystalline **1:** 14
  sound conduction **5:** 11, (46–47)
  strain **1:** 42–45
  strength **1:** 43–44
  vibrating **5:** 20–23, (50)
solid-state devices **9:** 20–23
  uses **9:** 32–35
solutions of ions **6:** 36–37, (50–51)
sonar
  bats **5:** *27*
  fishing **5:** *34–35*
  medicine **5:** 27
  seascape **5:** *34*
  ships **5:** 27
Sony Walkman **8:** *41*
soot **6:** 26–27
sound
  absorption **5:** 35
  amplification **8:** 31
  beaming **5:** *36,* 37
  compression **5:** 45
  electromagnetism **8:** 30–31
  energy **2:** *28, 29*
  human range **5:** 26
  loudness **5:** 32–33
  materials **5:** 25, 30–31
  noise **5:** *6–7, 9*
  pitch **5:** *11, 12*
  pure **5:** *39*
  qualities **5:** 9
  range of **5:** 28–29
  reflection **5:** 34–35
  refraction **5:** 36–37
  speed **5:** 10–11, 24–25, 25, **6:** 24
  string orchestra **5:** *12*
  timbre (color) **5:** 9, 14
  as vibration **5:** 7
sound broadcasting **7:** 38–41, **9:** 13
sound conduction **5:** 7–9, (46)
  compressed air **5:** (46)
  speed **5:** 10–11, 25, (46–47)
sound delay **5:** 25, 34, 35
sound frequency range **5:** 28–29
sound intensity
  distance **5:** 36–37
  energy **5:** 32–33
sound recording **8:** 31
sound shaping, mouth **5:** 41
sound waves **5:** 6–9
  properties **5:** 10–11
  solid **5:** 30–31
  thunder **6:** 24
south pole **8:** 12, *13*
south-seeking pole **8:** 9, 23
space probe, power supply **4:** *9*
space radiation **9:** 15
space satellite *see* satellite
space shuttle **2:** *10,* **9:** *35*
spark gap **7:** 36
spark plug **1:** 34
speaker identification **5:** 41
special effects **9:** 41
specific heat capacity **3:** 16–17
spectrographs **6:** 16
spectrum of light **4:** 22–23
speech machinery **5:** *41*
speed **2:** 21
speed of light **4:** 12–13
speed of sound **5:** 10–11, 24–25, 36, **6:** 24
speedometer **8:** *20*
spherical aberration **4:** 33, *39*
spiders **5:** *29*
spin drier **2:** (50)
spinning water **2:** (50–51)
split-ring commutator **8:** 35
sponge **1:** 13
spoon, chiming **5:** (50–51)
spraygun **1:** 32, **6:** 27, *28*
spring balance **2:** 12–13
springy lever **2:** *36*
squirrel-cage **8:** 36–37
SRAM **9:** 29
stability **2:** 32–33, 32–35
  center of gravity **2:** 33, *35*
  equilibrium **2:** 32–35
standard form **2:** 9
standard of living **9:** 40–45
Stanford Linear Accelerator Center **10:** 26
star angle measurement **2:** *8*
starlight, simulated **4:** *45*
stars **10:** *42*
starter relay, car **8:** 30, *31*
static electricity **6:** 6–7, **7:** 6, 9
  attraction **6:** (48–49)
  balloons **6:** (48–49)
  comb **6:** 7, 9, 26, (46–47), **7:** 6, 9
  dust removal **6:** 26–27
  friction **6:** 31
  generator **6:** 19, 20
  liquids **6:** 27
  photocopier **6:** 28–29
  positive/negative **6:** 8
  principle **6:** 26–29
  repulsion **6:** (48–49)
  uses **6:** 26–29
static friction **2:** *41*
static RAM **9:** 29
stator
  DC motor **8:** *36*
  generators **7:** 23
  induction motor **8:** 36
steam **1:** 22, 23, 28, 32, **7:** 23
steam engine **1:** *32–33,* 33–34
steel **1:** 18, 19, 21, 44
  expansion **3:** *25*
  magnetic attraction **8:** (48–49)
  thermal conductivity **3:** *28*
steelmaking **7:** 28
steering wheel **2:** 39
stock exchange **9:** *40,* 41–42
stone **1:** 44
stopping **5:** 13
  electric motor **8:** 40–41
storage
  charge **6:** 17, *21,* **7:** 12–13
  computer **9:** 28–31
storage heater **3:** 17
strain **1:** 42–45, **2:** 27, *28*
straws, Pan pipes **5:** (47)
streamlining **1:** 38–39, 41
streetcars **8:** 44
streetlight control **4:** 9
strength
  electromagnets **8:** (51)
  magnets **8:** (46)
  materials **1:** 19–20, 43–44
stress **1:** *44*
string orchestra **5:** *12*
strings, vibrating **5:** 12–15
  harmonics **5:** 14, *15*
  length **5:** 13
  pitch **5:** 13, 14
  resonance **5:** 29
  tension **5:** 13
  weight **5:** 14
stroking, magnetization **8:** 7, 16, *17*
Styrofoam **3:** 29
subatomic particles **10:** 17, 18
sublimation **3:** 18
submarines **1:** 21, 39, **10:** 38
submersible **1:** 21
subsonic vibration **5:** 28–31
substation **7:** *20,* 21, 24
subtractive process **4:** 27–28
sugar molecules **1:** 15
sugar solution **6:** 37
sugars, photosynthesis **4:** 8
sulfur **1:** 15
sulfuric acid **6:** 40
Sun
  angle measurement **2:** *8*
  eclipse **4:** 10–11
  energy **3:** 37, **4:** 8
  fusion reactions **10:** *43*
  heat **3:** 9, *38*
  magnetic field **8:** 15
  nuclear energy **10:** 42–43
  particles, charged **10:** 42–43
  plasma **10:** 44
  pressure **10:** 42–43
  slow setting **4:** *19,* 20
  temperature **1:** 23, **6:** 24
  see also entries beginning solar
  x-ray photograph **3:** *38*
sundial **2:** *8,* **8:** *7*
sunlight
  energy conversion **4:** 8–9
  spectrum **4:** 22–23
supercomputer **9:** *33,* 34
superconductivity **1:** 31, **3:** 45, **7:** 17
  electromagnets **8:** 21, *43,* **8:** 45
  high temperature **7:** 17
  theory **9:** 18
supercooling **1:** 30
SuperDrive disk **9:** 30
superfluidity **3:** 45
supermarket checkout **9:** *44*
supernova **10:** *6, 7*
supersonic boom **5:** *24*
supersonic sound *see* ultrasound
supersonic vibrations **5:** 26–27
surface tension **1:** 13, (50–51)
surfaces, curved **1:** 38–39, (51)
surfactant **1:** 13
surfing **6:** *36*
Swan, Joseph **4:** 7
sweating **1:** 24
swinging pendulum *see* pendulum
switches **7:** *30,* (48–49)
synchronous motor **8:** 41
synchrotron **10:** *26,* 26–27
Szilard, Leo **10:** 28–29

T

Tacoma Narrows **5:** 30
tape, demagnetization **8:** 16
tape player **8:** *41*
tape recording **5:** 43–44
tape storage **9:** 30, 36
telecommunications **7:** 41, **9:** 42
  see also radio communications; satellite communications; telegraphy; telephone
telegraphy **7:** 32–33, **8:** 29–30
  wireless **7:** 36–37
telephone **7:** 34–35
  mobile **7:** 39–40, 41, **9:** 42
  optical cables **4:** 21
  routing **7:** 35
  satellite **9:** 42
telephoto lens **4:** 37
teleprinter **7:** 33
telescope **4:** 37–39
television **7:** 42–45
  color **7:** 43–45
  color production **4:** 26
  Crookes tube **9:** 9
  global **7:** *42*
  high-definition **7:** 45
  interactive **7:** 45
  intercontinental **9:** 40–41
  mechanical **7:** 43
  picture flicker **7:** *44,* 45
television camera **7:** 43–44
television receiver **4:** 26, **7:** *43,* 44–45
television tube **6:** 32, **7:** *43,* 45, **8:** 21, 26–27
  see also cathode-ray tube
temperature **1:** 11, 23, 27, 29, **3:** 7
  atomic vibration **3:** 7
  color **3:** 36
  conduction rate **3:** 29
  electrical conductivity **9:** 17
  hotness **3:** 10–11, *17*
  human body **3:** 13
  infrared **3:** 35–36
  measuring **3:** 12–15
  Ohm's law **7:** 14, 15
  scale **3:** 10–11
  scale conversions **3:** 15
  speed of sound **5:** 25, 36
  Sun's surface **6:** 24
  and viscosity **3:** (46)
temple doors **3:** *23*
tennis court **9:** (46–47)
tension **1:** 44
  drumskin **5:** 21
  and frequency **5:** 13
tera- (prefix) **2:** *9*
terminal speed **2:** 14–15
TGV **8:** *44–45*
Thales **6:** 6, 7
theater, acoustics **5:** 35
thermal conduction rate **3:** 28–29
thermal conductivity **3:** *28,* 29, (48–49)
thermal lance **3:** *10*
thermals **3:** 30, *32*
thermionic emission **6:** 31, *32,* **9:** 10
thermocouple **3:** *12,* 15
thermodynamic temperature **3:** 11
thermograph **3:** *34,* 35
thermometer **3:** 12–15
  alcohol **3:** 13
  bimetallic strip **3:** 14
  clinical **3:** 13
  crystals **3:** *13*
  digital **3:** *12*
  liquid expansion **3:** 20–21, (47)
  liquid-in-glass **3:** *12,* 13
  low-temperature **3:** 13
  maximum and minimum **3:** *15*
  mercury **3:** *12,* 13
  platinum resistance **3:** *12,* 15
  pyrometer **3:** *15*
  scales **3:** 10–11
  thermocouple **3:** *12*
thermos flask **3:** 39–40
thermostat **3:** *14*

Thompson, Benjamin (Count Rumford) **3:** 9
  heat from friction **3:** 8–9
Thomson, J. J. **6:** 31, **9:** 6, **10:** *6*, 10
Thomson, William (Lord Kelvin) **3:** 11
thorium **10:** 16, 19, *21*
Three Mile Island **10:** 33–34
Thrust 2 **5:** *24*
thunder 5: 29, **6:** 22–25
tightrope **2:** *35*, **5:** *38*
timbre **5:** 9, 14
time delay, satellites **7:** 41
time measurement **2:** *8*
timpani **5:** 21, *22*, 23
tokamak fusion reactor **10:** *43, 44*, 45
Tokyo stock exchange **9:** *40*
toner, photocopying **6:** 29
tongue, sound production **5:** 41
toothed wheels *see* cogs
torque **2:** *35*, **7:** 12, **8:** 33, 34–35
  see also turning moment
Torricelli, Evangelista **1:** 8
torsion balance **2:** *13*
torus **10:** 45
total internal reflection **4:** 21
tracer **10:** 23
trachea **5:** 40, *41*
trading, electronic **9:** *40*, 41–42
train
  diesel-electric **8:** 44
  electric **7:** *8*, **8:** 44–45
  maglev **3:** 45, **8:** *42, 43*, 45
  steam **1:** *32–33*, 33–34
  TGV **8:** *44–45*
transducer, ultrasound **5:** 27
transformer **7:** 20–21, 23–24
transistor
  amplification **9:** 22, 23
  field-effect **9:** *21, 22*, 23
  integrated circuit **9:** 25–27
  invention **9:** 18, 19
  junction **9:** *21*, 22
  size **9:** *23*
transmitter **7:** *39*
trap-door spider **5:** *29*
trash, recycling **6:** 13
tree, stability **2:** *33*
tremolo **5:** 13
triangle of vectors **2:** 17
Trinitron CRT **7:** *43*, 44
triode **9:** *10*, 11, 13, 19
tritium
  fusion **10:** *43*, (51)
  neutrons **10:** 9
  tokamak **10:** 45
  Urey, H. **10:** 12–13
trombone **5:** 19
truck **3:** 40, **9:** *14*
trumpet **5:** 19
trusses **1:** 44
tuba **5:** 19
tubes, vacuum 9: 10–11
  semiconductor **9:** 19
thermionic emission
  6: 31, *32*, **9:** 10
  uses 9: 12–13
tumor detection **3:** 35
tungsten **1:** 23, 26
  filament **7:** 18, 19
  light filament **4:** 7
  x-rays **6:** 33
tuning, glass bells **5:** (49)
tuning fork **5:** *39*
tunneling electron micrograph **9:** *6*
turbine **1:** 35
  boiling-water reactors **10:** 36
  generator **7:** 9
  nuclear energy **10:** *37*
turboalternator **7:** *22*
turbogenerator **7:** 23
turbulence **1:** 39, 41
turning moment **2:** 34–35
  balance **2:** 34
  coil **8:** *33*
  couples **2:** 34–35
  wrench **2:** 34, *35*
  see also torque
twist *see* torque
two-pole motor **8:** 40
Tyndall, John **1:** 27

U

UHF **7:** 37, 38–39, 39, **9:** 42
ultracapacitors **8:** 43
ultrasound **5:** 26, 27
ultraviolet light **3:** *36–37*, **6:** 32, *33*, 35, **9:** 26
undersea mapping **5:** *35*
underwater fountain **3:** (49)
unit (kilowatt-hour) **7:** 16
units
  mass/weight, conversion between **2:** 12
  prefixes **2:** 7, 9
  SI system **2:** *7*, 9
  standard form **2:** 9
  standardization **2:** 6–7
unstable equilibrium **2:** 32–33
unvoiced sounds **5:** 40
upthrust **1:** 20
uranium **10:** 19
  atom **1:** *6*, 17
  chain reaction **10:** 29, 30–31
  depleted **10:** 40
  enriched **10:** 31, 40–41
  fission **10:** 29, 32
  fluorine **10:** 13
  nucleus **10:** 28–29, (46)
  supplies **10:** 38, 40
uranium hexafluoride **10:** 13
uranium isotopes
  fast breeder reactor **10:** *33*
  nuclear bombs **10:** *12*, 13
  radioactivity **10:** 11, 16, 20, *21*
Urey, Harold **10:** 12–13

V

vacuum bottle **3:** 39–40
vacuum tubes 9: 10–11
  uses 9: 12–13
valves **1:** 34, 37
Van Allen belts **8:** 14
Van de Graaff, Robert **6:** 20
Van de Graaff generator **6:** 20–21
van Leeuwenhoek, Anton **4:** 39
vaporization **1:** 23, 24–25, *31*, 32, **3:** 18, *19*, 42
variation **8:** 12
vectors 2: 16–17
  acceleration as **2:** 21
  addition **2:** 17
  force **6:** 10
vehicles, electric 6: *42*, **7:** 29, **8:** 42–45
velocity **2:** 21, 22
VHF **7:** 37, 38–39
vibraphone **5:** *21*
vibration
  columns of air 5: 16–19, (47)
  resonance **5:** 29–30
  skins 5: 20–23, (48), (48–49)
  solids 5: 20–23, (50)
  sound waves **5:** 7–8, *9*
  strings 5: 12–15
  subsonic 5: 28–31
  supersonic 5: 26–27
video camera **7:** *45*
videotape **8:** 16, 19, **9:** 41
vinyl records **5:** 42, 43
virtual focus **4:** 16
virtual image **4:** 15, 17
viscosity **1:** 13, **3:** (46)
vision, defects **4:** 35
vocal cords **5:** 40
voice, human 5: 40–41
voicebox (larynx) **5:** 40, *41*
voiced sounds **5:** 40
voiceprints **5:** 41
volcano **1:** *26*, **3:** *9*, **5:** *35*
volt **2:** *7*
Volta, Alessandro **6:** 20, 42, *43*
voltage **7:** 8–11, 10
  domestic **7:** 25
  induced **7:** 20–21
  power **7:** 18
  see also potential difference
voltage, high **6:** *18*, 19, 20–21
  neon **6:** 32
  spark **6:** 35
  x-rays **6:** 33
voltage change *see* transformer
voltage-time graph, AC/DC **7:** *21*
voltaic pile **6:** 43
volume **1:** 11, 18, 28–29
volume
  expansion/expansivity
  gas **3:** 22–23
  liquids **3:** 20–22
  solids **3:** 25
vowels **5:** 40

W

Walkman **8:** *41*
Walton, Ernest **10:** 24, *25*
waste, radioactive **7:** 26
watches **8:** 41, **9:** 41
water **1:** 6
  anomalous expansion **3:** 21–22
  boiling point **1:** 23, **3:** *11*
  change of state **3:** 18, *19*
  conductor **6:** (50)
  cooling **7:** 23
  density **1:** 18–19, 30
  deuterium **10:** *9*
  displacement **1:** 20, 21, (47)
  electrolysis **6:** 39, **10:** 13
  expansion **3:** (47)
  fire fighting **1:** *12, 36*
  freezing point **3:** *11*
  gases **6:** 39
  heavy **10:** *8, 9*, 31, 32, (49–50)
  hydrogen **10:** *9*
  ice **1:** 30
  latent heat **3:** 18, *19*
  as lens **4:** (50), (50–51)
  meniscus **1:** 13
  molecular structure **6:** 37
  nuclear reactor coolant **10:** 31, *34*, 36
  oxygen **10:** *9*
  polar solvent **6:** 37
  purification **1:** *31*
  specific heat capacity **3:** 16, *17*
  superheated **10:** *33, 39*
  viscosity **1:** 13
  volume expansivity **3:** 21
water boatman **1:** *13*
water bomber **1:** *12*
water clock **2:** *8*
water cycle **1:** 25
water droplets **1:** 28, 30, *31*
water mirage **4:** *20*
water vapor **1:** 31
watt **2:** *7*, 31
Watt, James **1:** 33
waveform rectification *see* rectifier
wavelength **5:** 10, *11*, **9:** (48–49)
  apparent **5:** 25
  energy **3:** *36*
  human perception **5:** 38
  infrared **3:** 40, *41*
  light **4:** 42
wave-power **7:** 26
waves
  drawing **9:** (48–49)
  earthquake **5:** 30–31
waves (sound), properties **5:** 10–11
waxes **1:** 14
weather **1:** *8*, 9, **3:** 30–31
wedge **2:** 40
weighing machines **2:** 12–13
weight 1: 8, 18, (47), **2:** 11–13
  falling objects **2:** (46–47)
  and mass 2: 11–13
  measuring **2:** 13
  pendulum swing **2:** (51)
  static friction **2:** *41*
weight (strings), and frequency **5:** 14
weightlifter **2:** *13*
welding **1:** 10
wetting agent **1:** 13
whales **5:** *25, 29*
Wheatstone, Charles **7:** 32
wheel and axle **2:** *38*, 39
wheelbarrow **2:** 36, *37*
Whispering Gallery **5:** *10*
white light
  color combining **4:** (47)
  fringes **4:** 43, *44*
  primary colors **4:** 26
  spectrum **4:** 22–23
wick **4:** 6–7
Wigner, Eugene **10:** 28–29
Wilson, C. T. R. **10:** 18
Wimshurst, James **6:** 19
Wimshurst machine **6:** 19, *20*
wind **1:** 11, **3:** 31
wind farm **7:** 26
wind resistance **2:** *21*
wind tunnels **1:** 41
wind turbine **7:** 26
winding gear **8:** *38*
windlass **2:** *38*, 39
windmills **1:** 11
window opener **1:** 27
windspeed, audibility **5:** *37*
wine bottle coolers **1:** 24–25
wing scales, butterfly **4:** *42*, 43
wire **1:** 15, 45
wireless telegraphy *see* telegraphy, wireless
wood **1:** 18, **3:** *28*
woodwind instruments **5:** *18*, 19, (48–49)
work 2: 27–31
wreck, sonar detection **5:** *34*
wrench **2:** 34, *35*

X

Xerox machines **6:** 28–29
x-rays 3: *36*, **6:** 20, **9:** 14–15
  Crookes tube **9:** 9
  crystals **1:** 17
  electromagnetic radiation **10:** 15
  high-voltages **6:** 33
  industrial components **10:** 22
  from space **9:** 15
  tube **9:** *15*
  tungsten **6:** 33
xylophone **5:** 21, (50)

Y

yield point **1:** 44–45

Z

zinc **6:** 35
zinc chloride **6:** 35
zircon **1:** *16*

Further Reading

General Reference

Albert Einstein and the Frontiers of Physics (Oxford Portraits in Science) by Jeremy Bernstein. Oxford University Press Children's Books

Basic Physics: A Self-Teaching Guide by Karl F. Kuhn. John Wiley & Sons

Essential Physics by Philippa Wingate. E D C Publications

Eyewitness Visual Dictionaries: Physics by Jack Challoner. DK Publishing

Great Scientific Discoveries (Chambers Compact Reference Series). Chambers

How Things Work: The Physics of Everyday Life by Louis A. Bloomfield. John Wiley & Sons

Illustrated Dictionary of Physics. E D C/Usborne

Introduction to Physics by Amanda Kent *et al.* E D C Publications

Janice Vancleave's Physics for Every Kid: 101 Easy Experiments in Motion, Heat, Light, Machines, and Sound (Science for Every Kid) by Janice Pratt VanCleave. John Wiley & Sons

Physics in the 20th Century by Curt Suplee *et al.* Harry N. Abrams

Physics Lab in the Home (Physical Science Labs) by Bob Fredhoffer. Franklin Watts

Physics Made Simple by Ira M. Freeman, William J. Durden (Designer). Doubleday Books

Physics Principles and Problems by Paul W. Zitzewitz. MacMillan Publishing Company

Physics: The Easy Way by Robert L. Lehrman. Barrons Educational Series

Science and Technology by Lisa Watts. E D C/Usborne

Science School by Mick Manning, Brita Granstrom (Illustrator). Kingfisher Books

The Flying Circus of Physics by Jearl Walker. John Wiley & Sons

The Kingfisher Science Encyclopedia, Editor Charles Taylor. Kingfisher Books

This Strange Quantum World & You by Patricia Topp. Blue Dolphin Publications

Turning the World Inside Out and 174 Other Simple Physics Demonstrations by Robert Ehrlich, Jearl Walker. Princeton University Press

Websites

The Children's Science Center – http://www.cyberstreet.com/csc/

How Stuff Works – http://www.howstuffworks.com

Science Laboratory – http://www.cbc4kids.ca/

The Why Files – http://whyfiles.news.wisc.edu/index.html

Mechanics

Awesome experiments in Force and Motion by Michael Anthony DiSpezio, Catherine Leary (Illustrator). Sterling Publications

Energy (Science Concepts) by Alvin Silverstein *et al.* Twenty First Century

Eyewitness Books: Force & Motion by Peter Lafferty. DK Publishing

Fatal Forces (Horrible Science) by Nick Arnold, Tony De Saulles (Illustrator). Scholastic Paperbacks

Forces and Movement (Straightforward Science) by Peter D. Riley. Franklin Watts

Isaac Newton and the Scientific Revolution (Oxford Portraits in Science) by Gale E. Christianson. Oxford University Press Children's Books

Mechanics Fundamentals: Funtastic Science Activities for Kids by Robert W. Wood, Bill Wright (Illustrator). McGraw-Hill

Newton and Gravity (Big Idea Series) by Paul Strathern. Doubleday

Physics Lab in a Hardware Store by Bob Friedhoffer, Joe Hosking (Illustrator). Franklin Watts

Sloppy Slimy Sticky Soggy Dripping Moving Science by Ray Miller, Michelle Morrow (Illustrator). Scholastic Paperbacks

What Makes Things Move? (First Science Books Series) by Althea and Robina Green (Illustrator). Troll Associates

Why Doesn't the Earth Fall Up? and Other Not Such Dumb Questions about Motion by Vicki Cobb *et al.* Lodestar Books

Photographic Acknowledgments

Abbreviations RHPL Robert Harding Picture Library SPL Science Photo Library

6 Andrew Syred/SPL; **8** Alexander Tsiaras/SPL; **9** RHPL; **10** NASA; **13 & 15** The Stock Market; **16** RHPL; **18** Leo Mason; **20-21** Quadrant Picture Library; **22** RHPL; **23** NASA; **24** James Stevenson/SPL; **25** SPL; **26** The Stock Market; **28** RHPL; **29** C. Bowman/RHPL; **30-31** RHPL; **32** Laguna Design/SPL; **33** A. Woolfitt/RHPL; **34** Image Select International; **35** Walter Rawlings/RHPL; **36** Professor Harold Edgerton/SPL; **38** RHPL; **39t** David Hughes/RHPL; **39b** Andromeda Oxford Limited; **40** The Stock Market; **42** Martin Bond/SPL; **44** Simon Harris/RHPL.

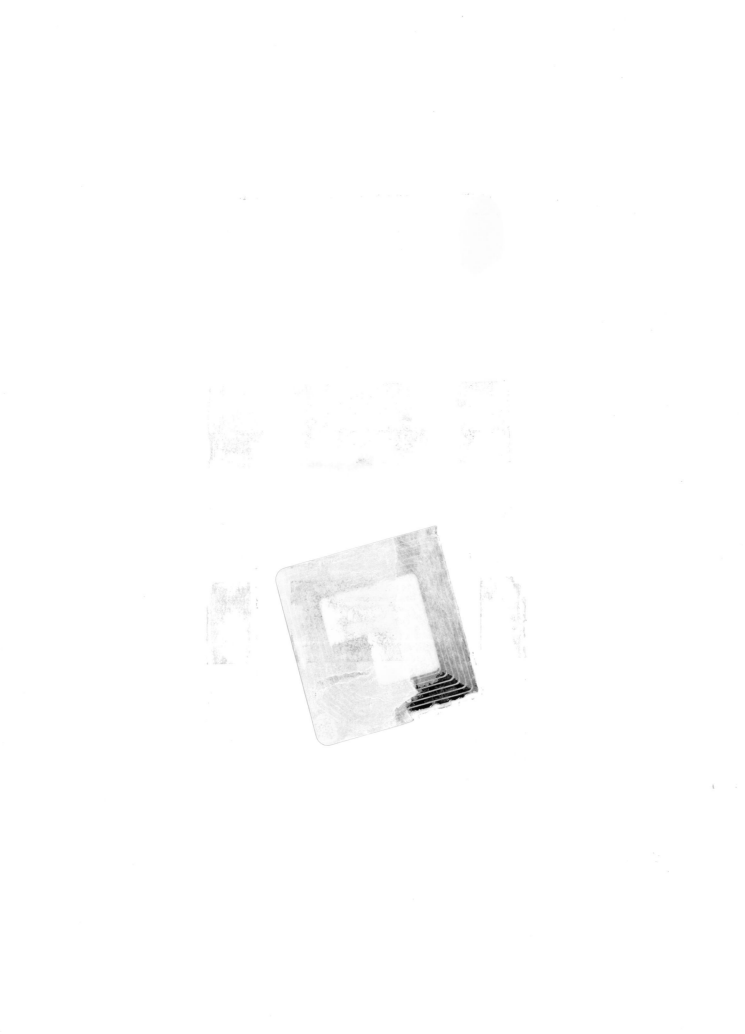